AF473954

DIVE DARK

DREAM SLOW

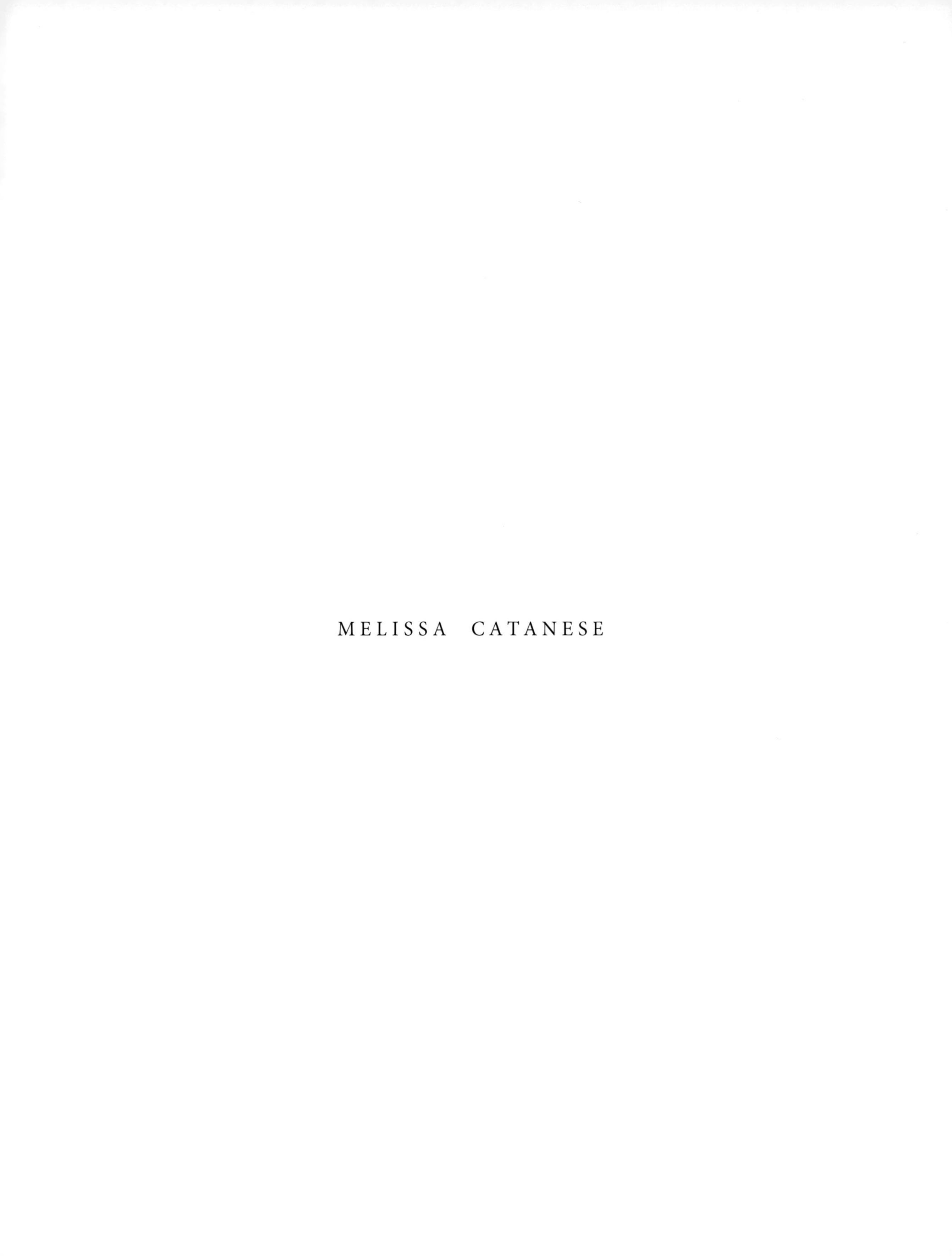

MELISSA CATANESE

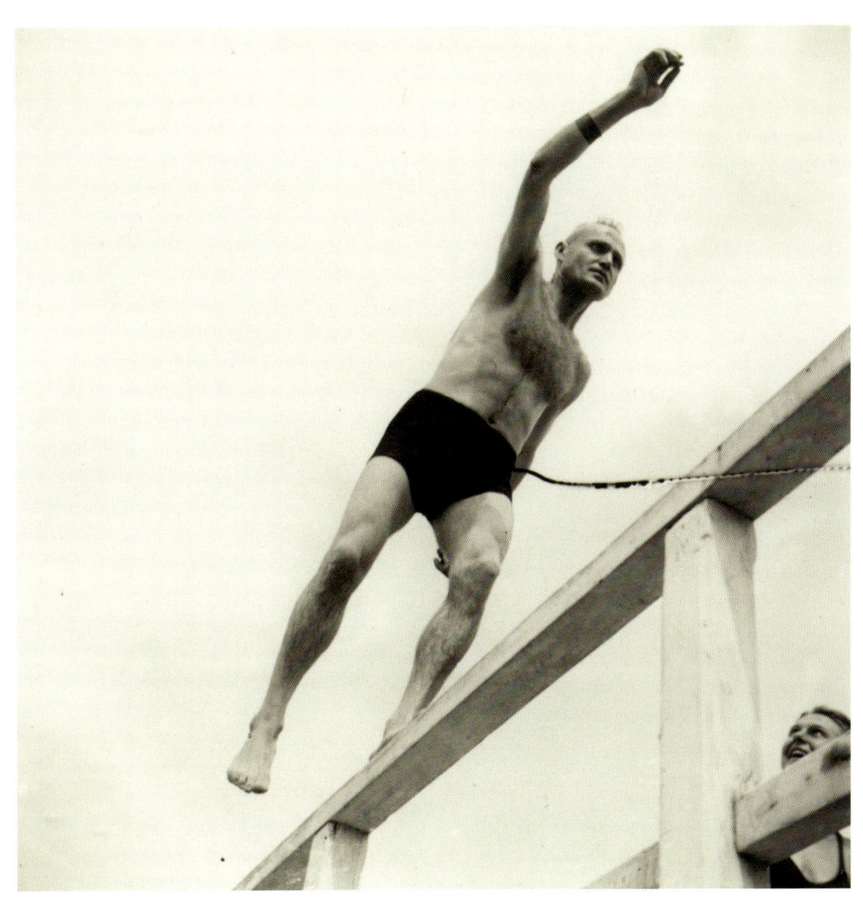

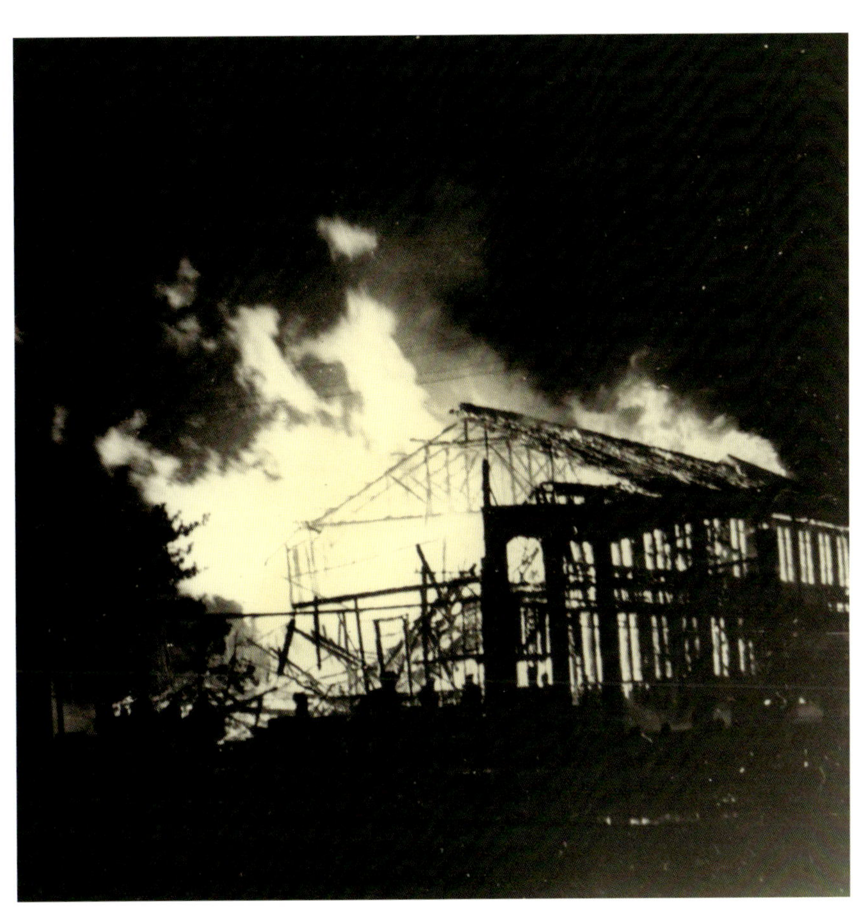

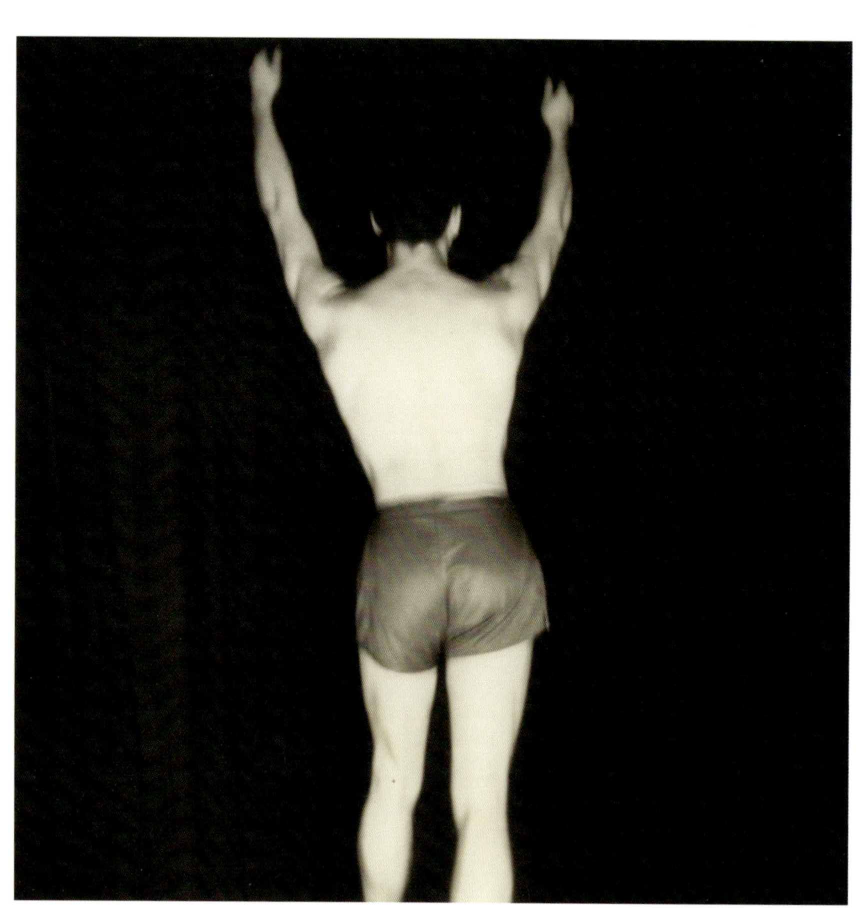

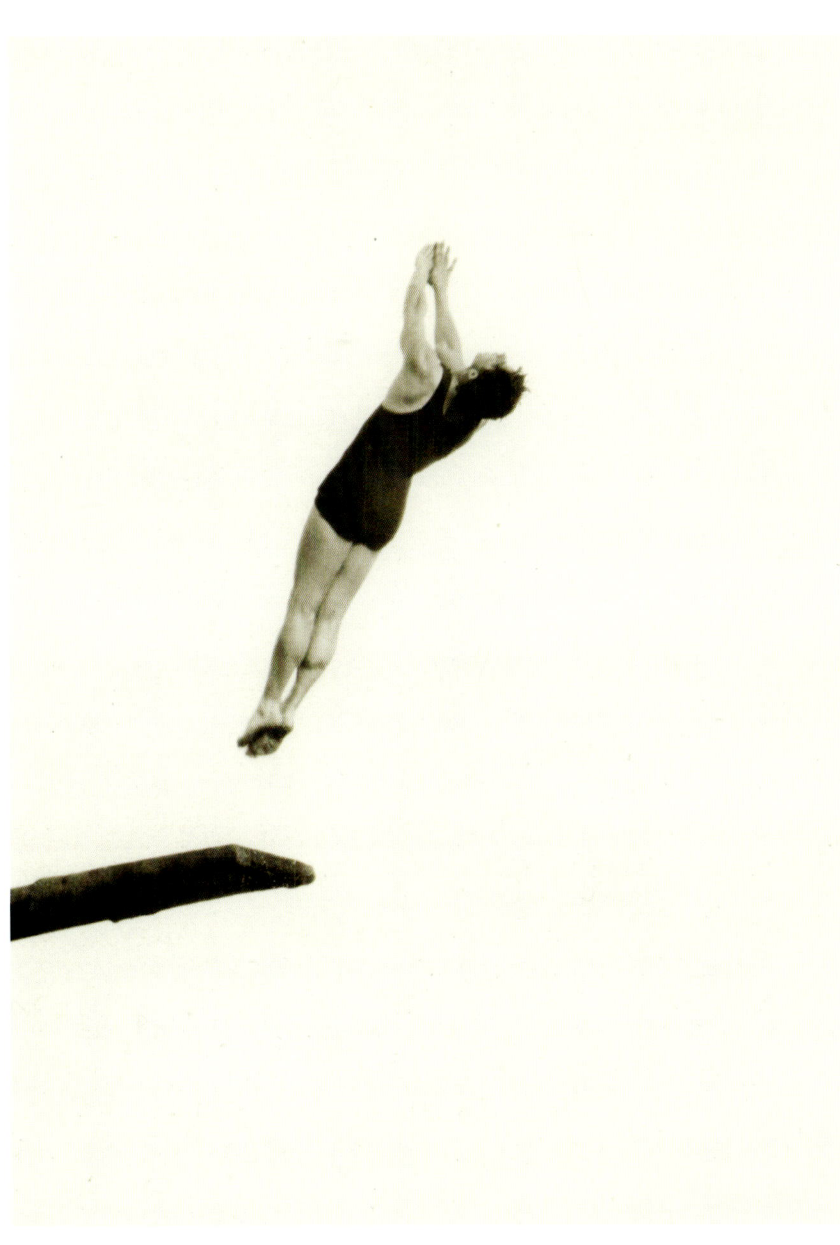

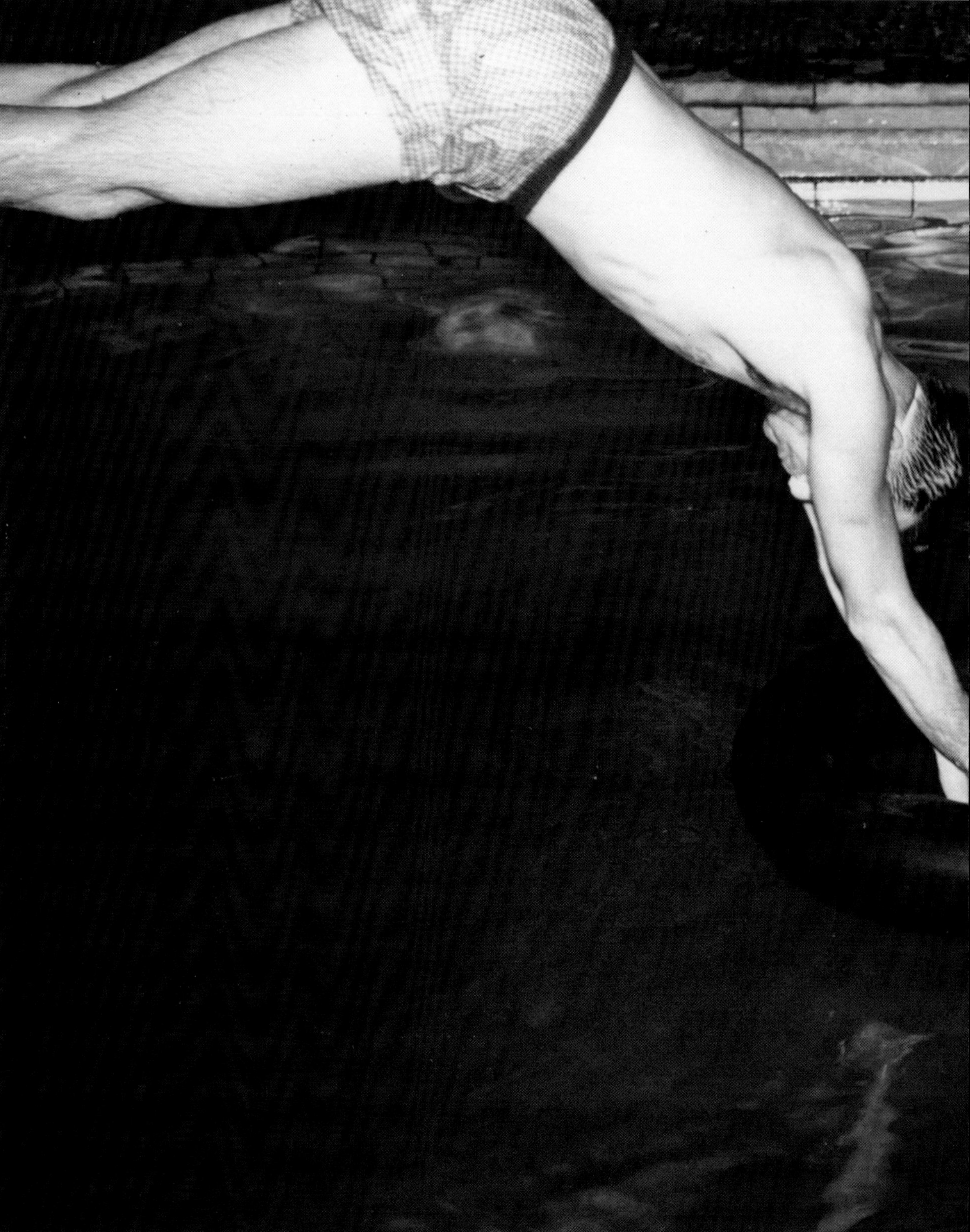

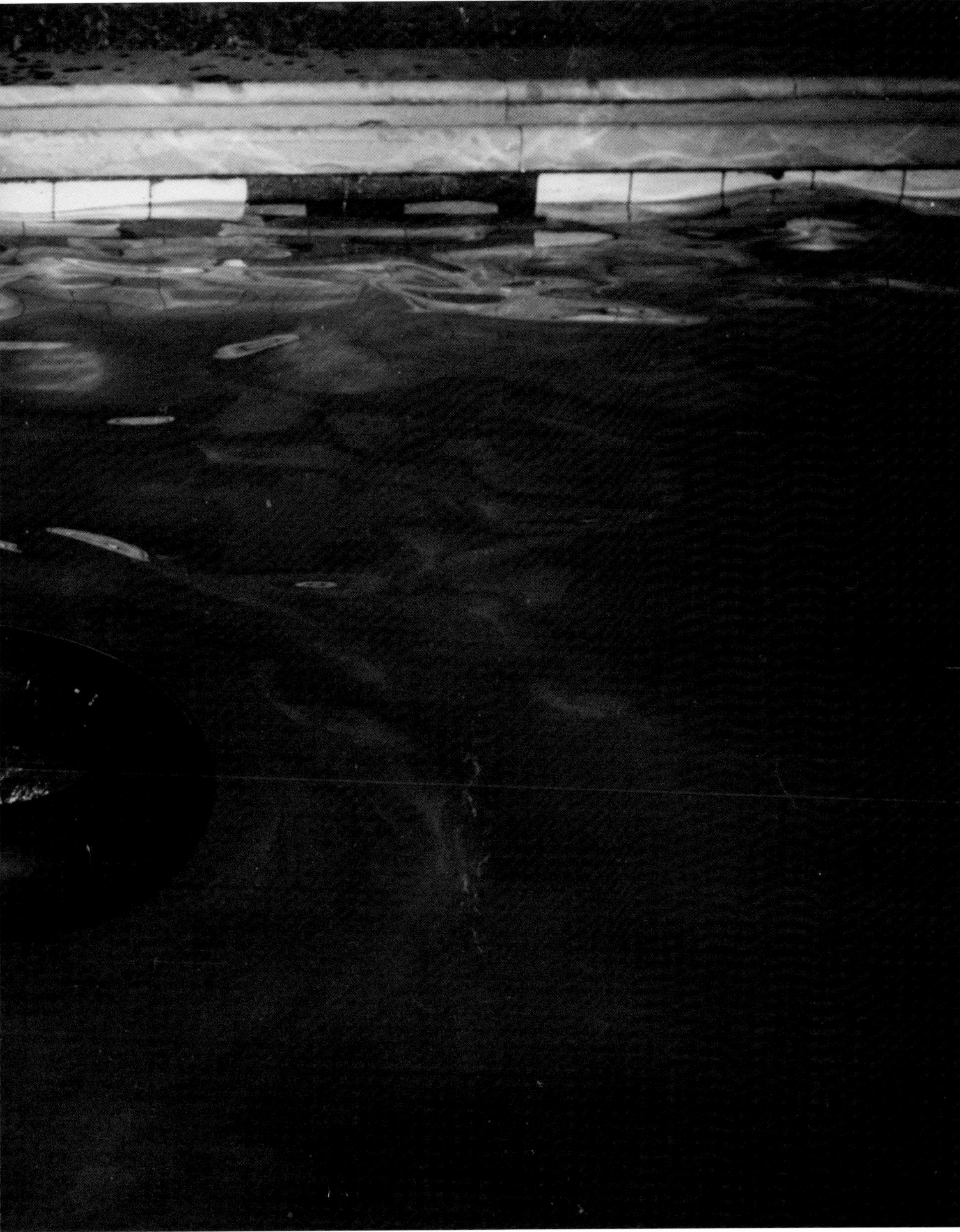

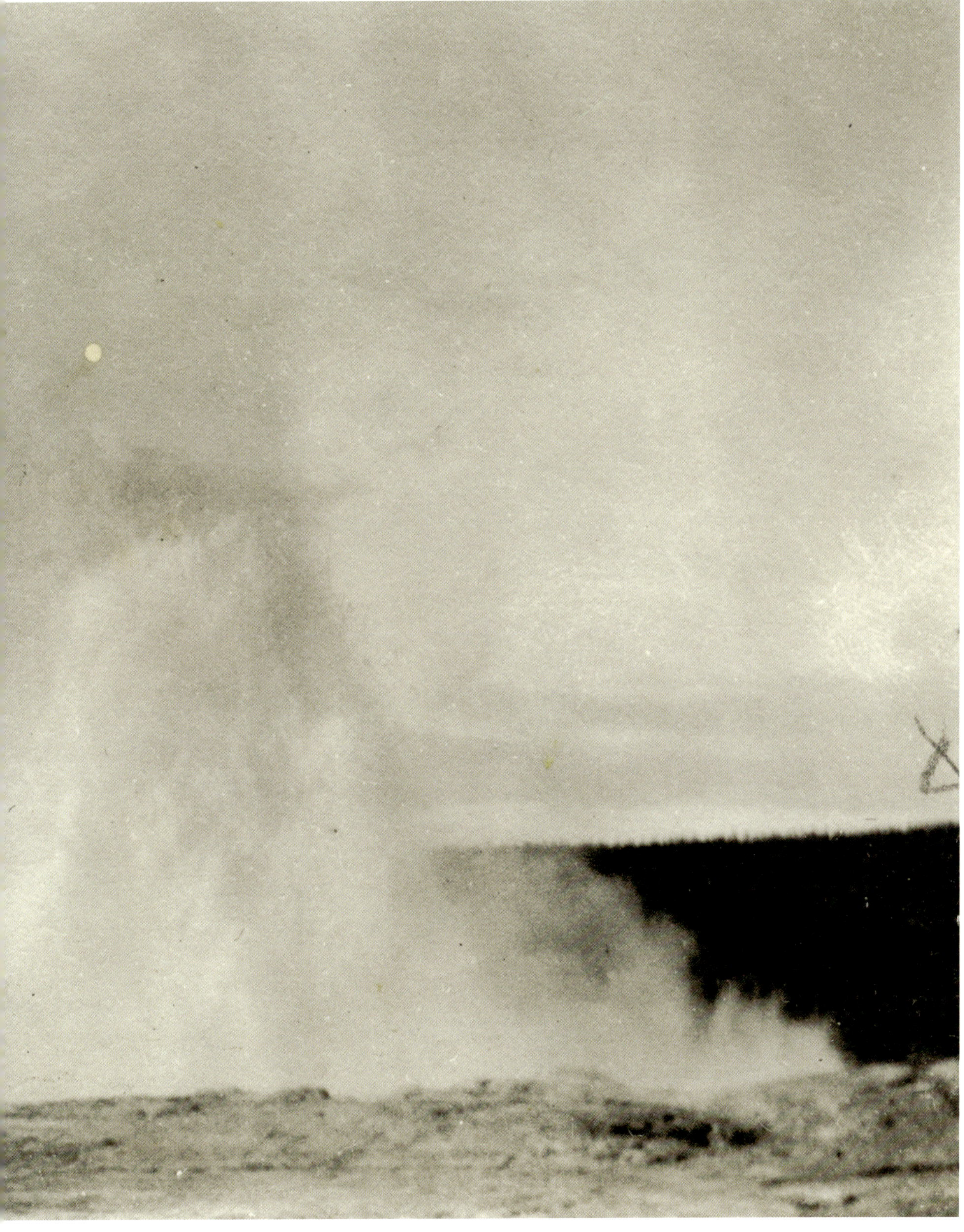

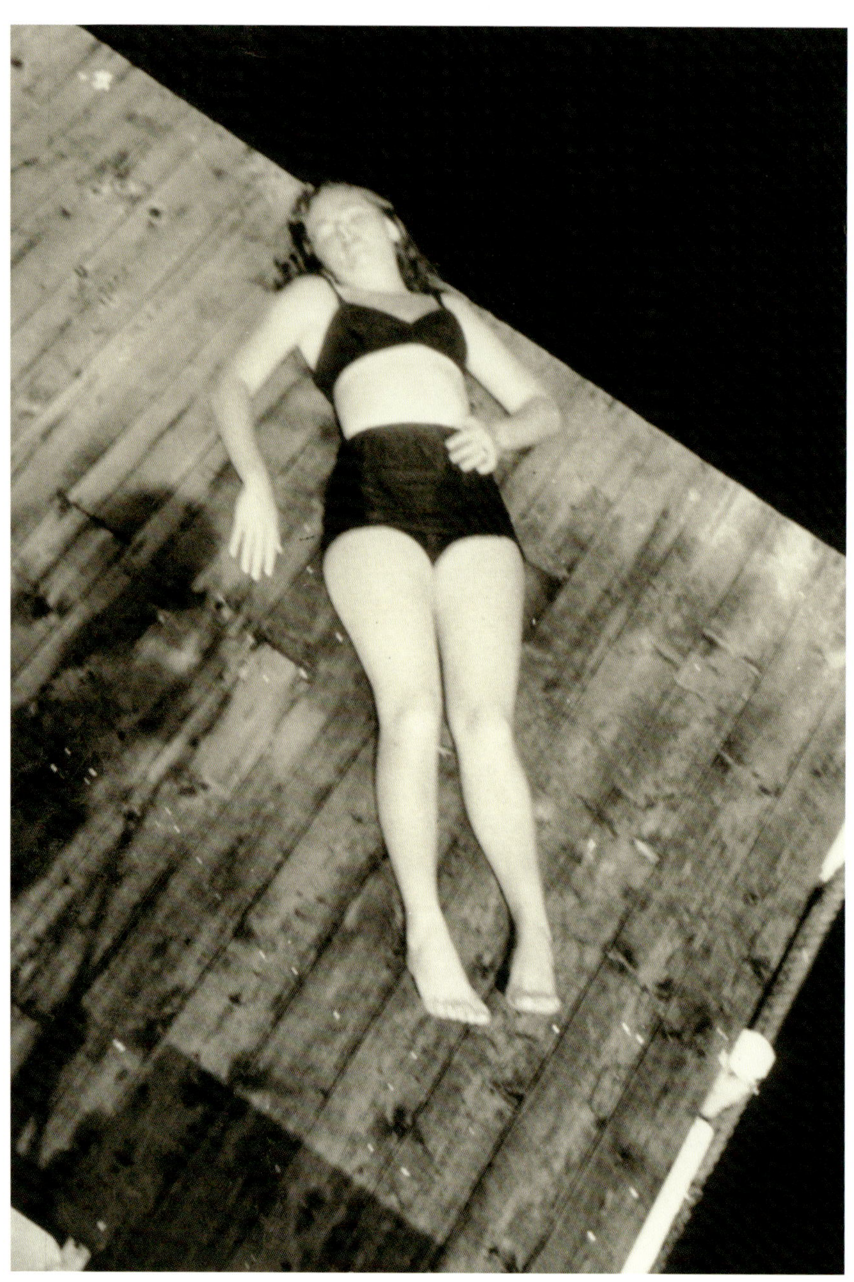

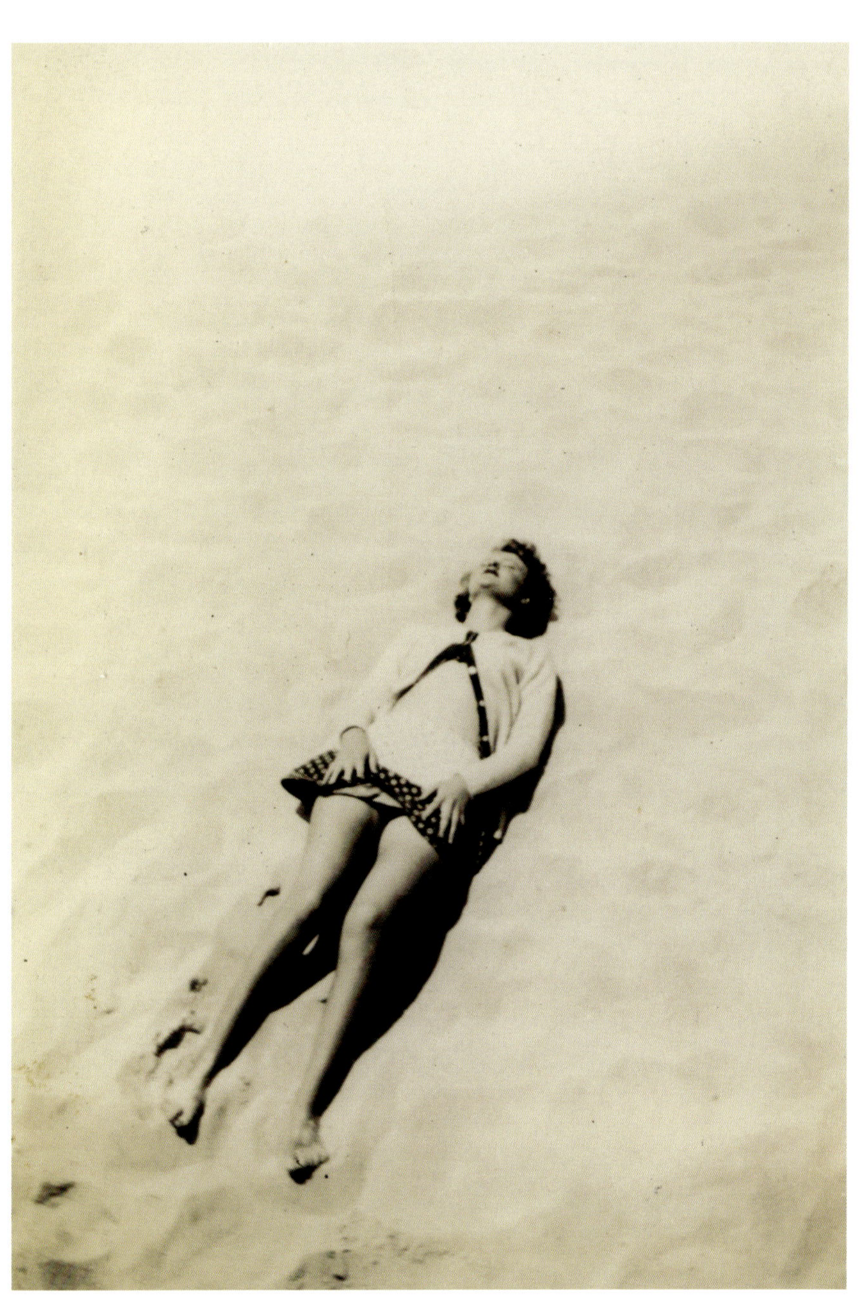

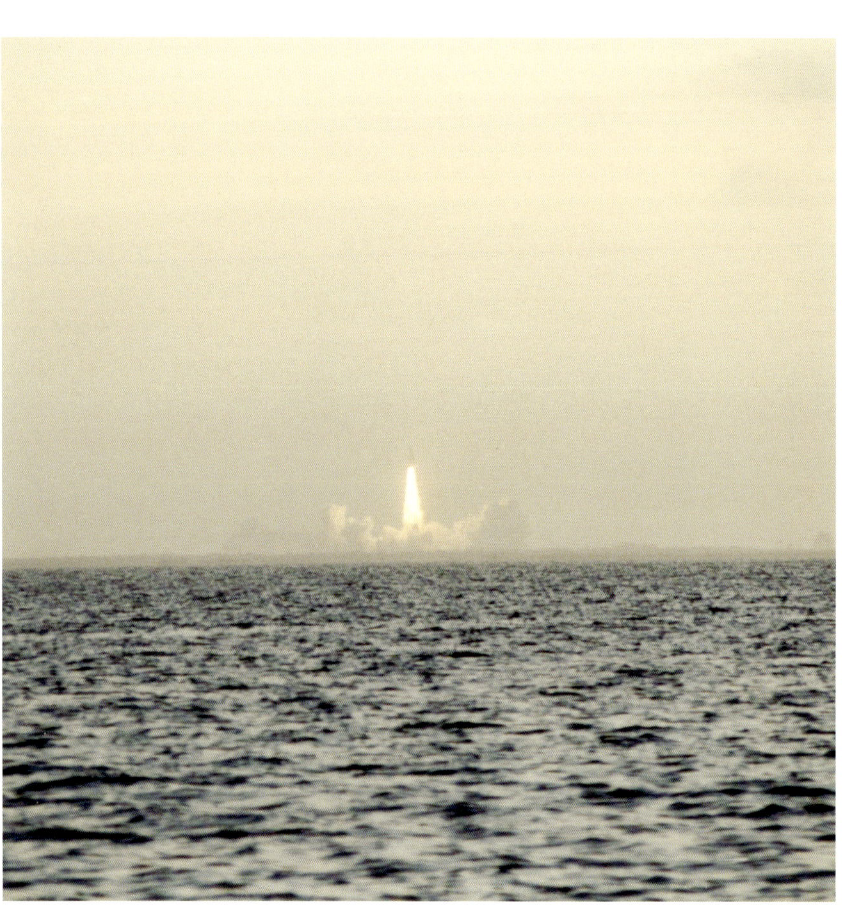

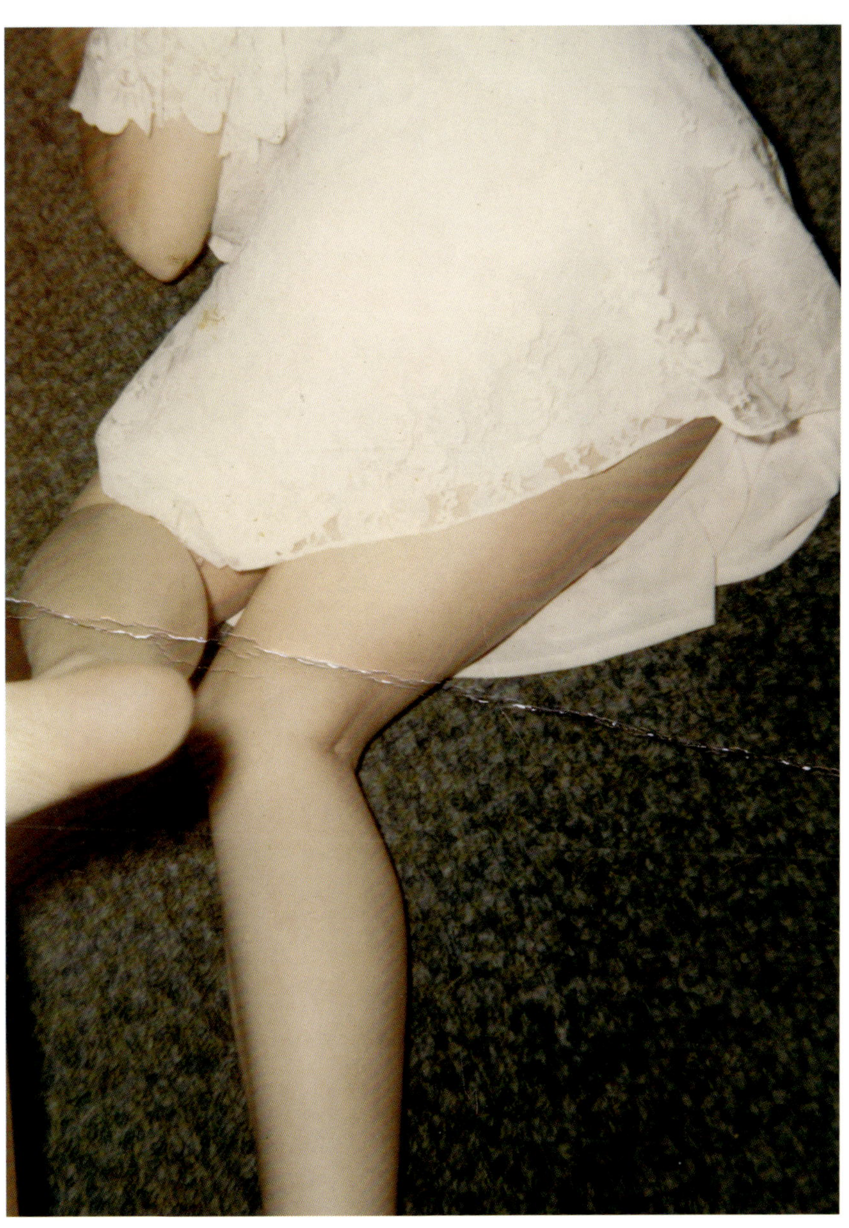

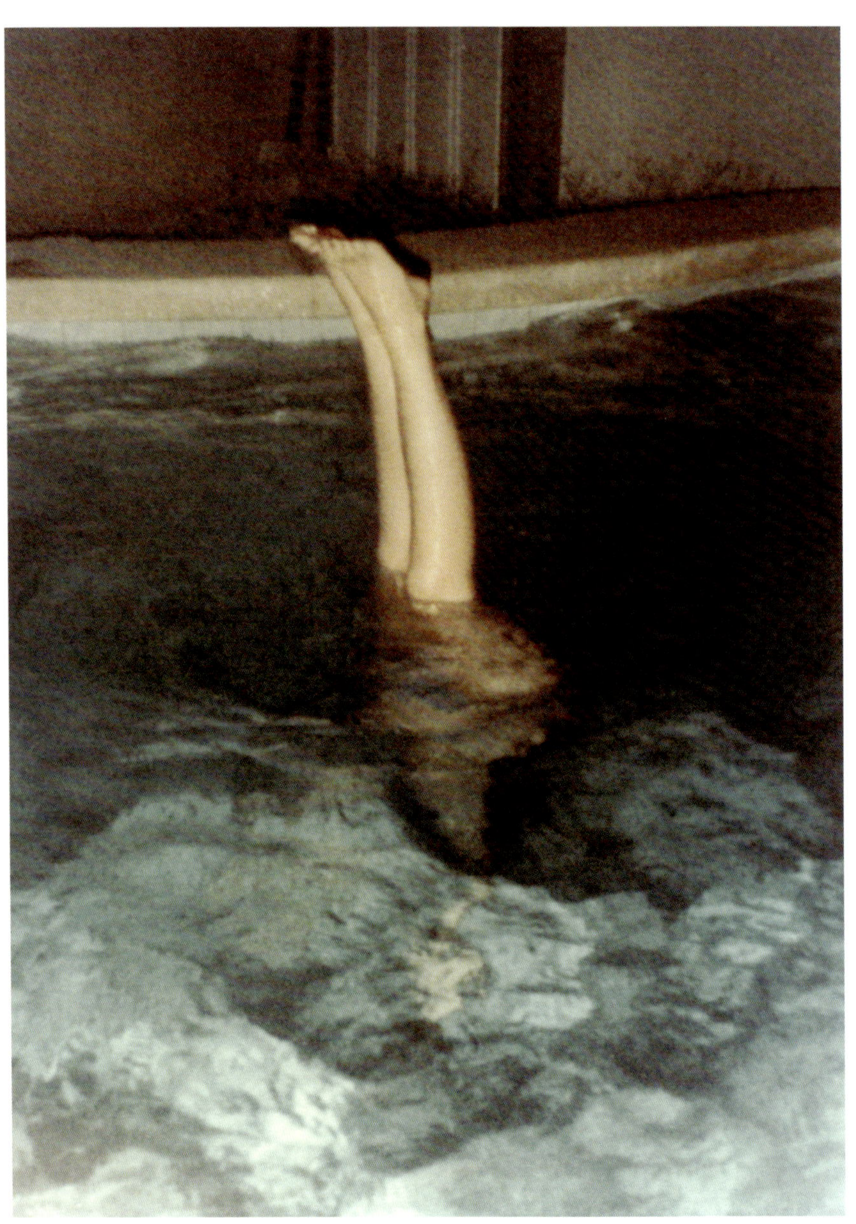

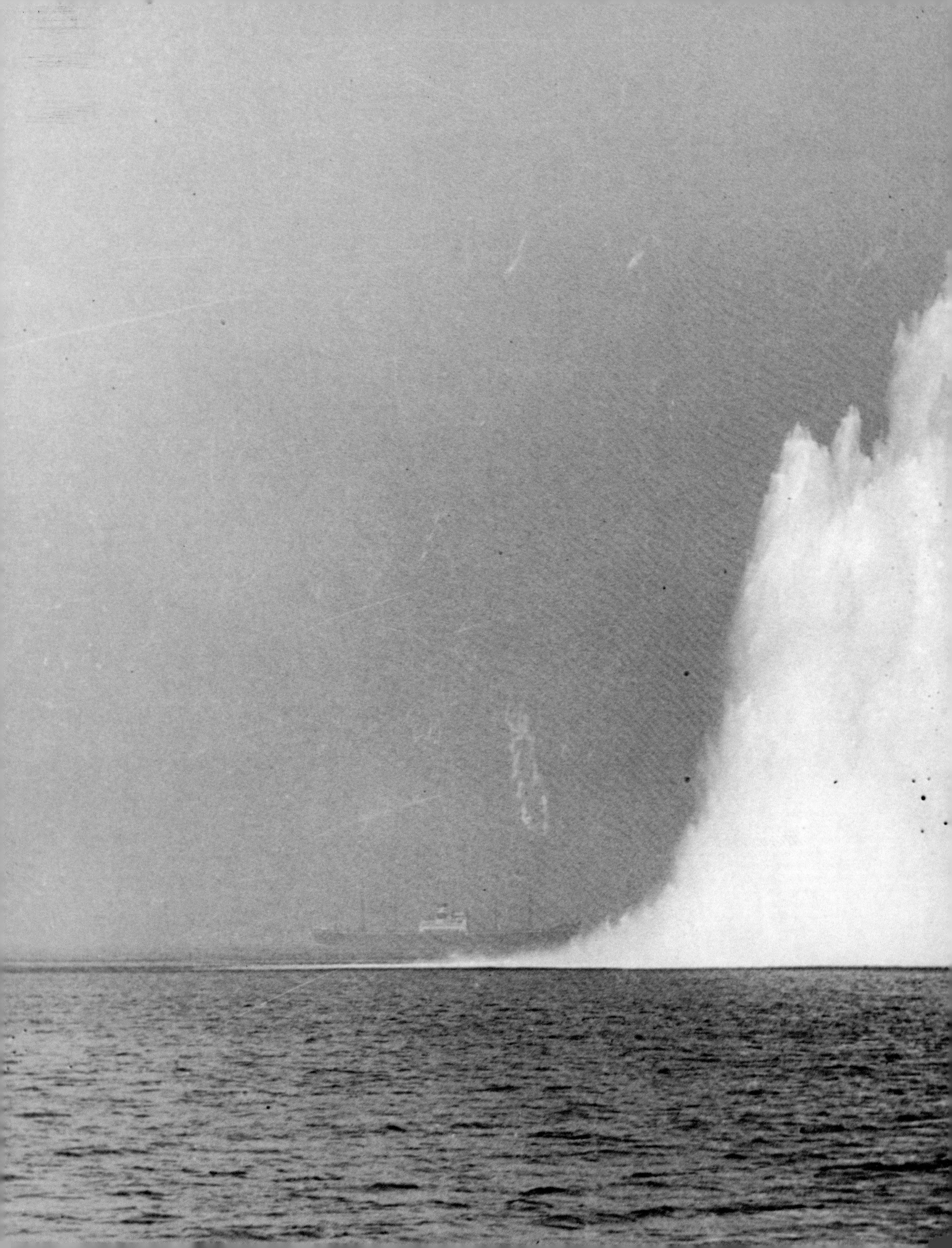

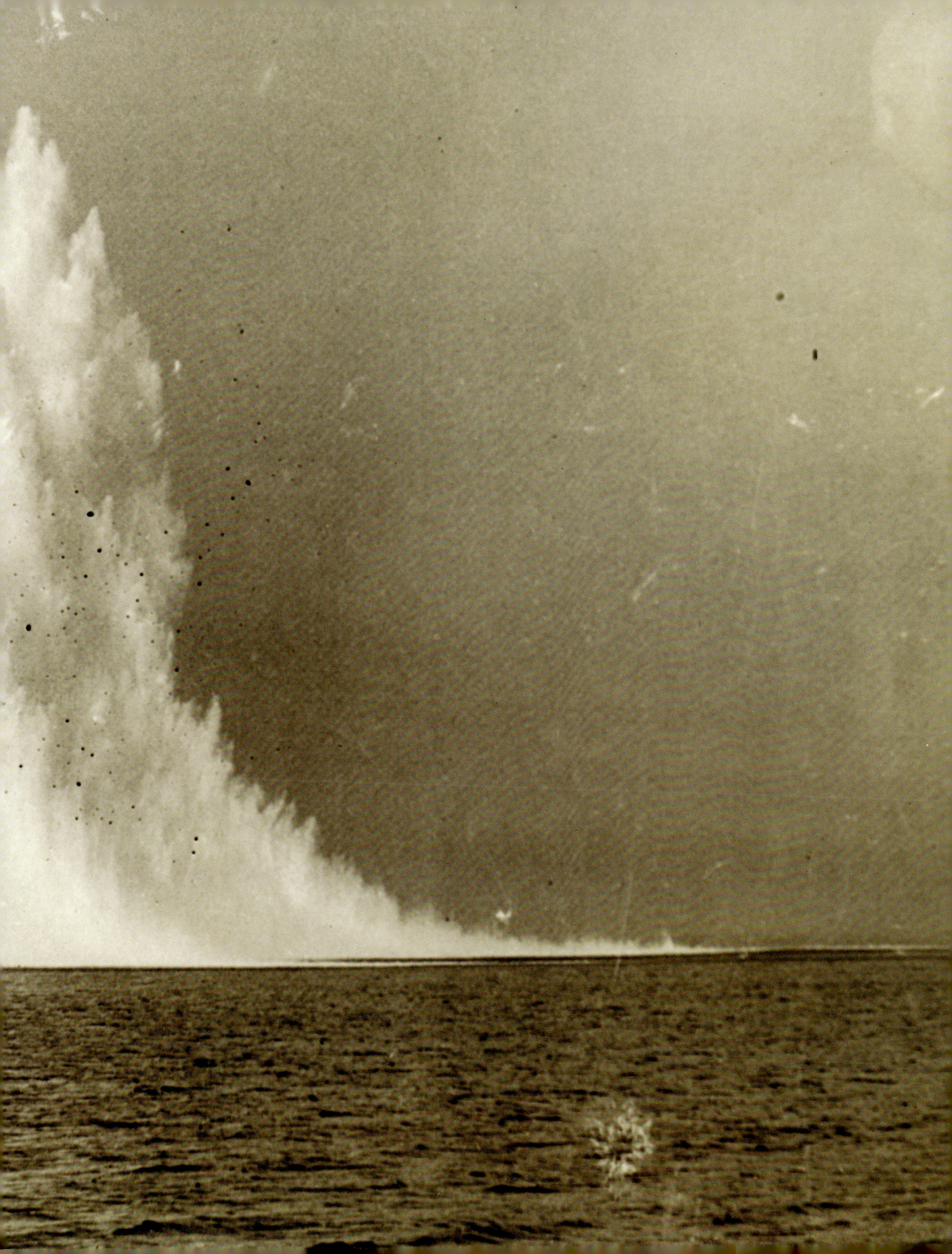

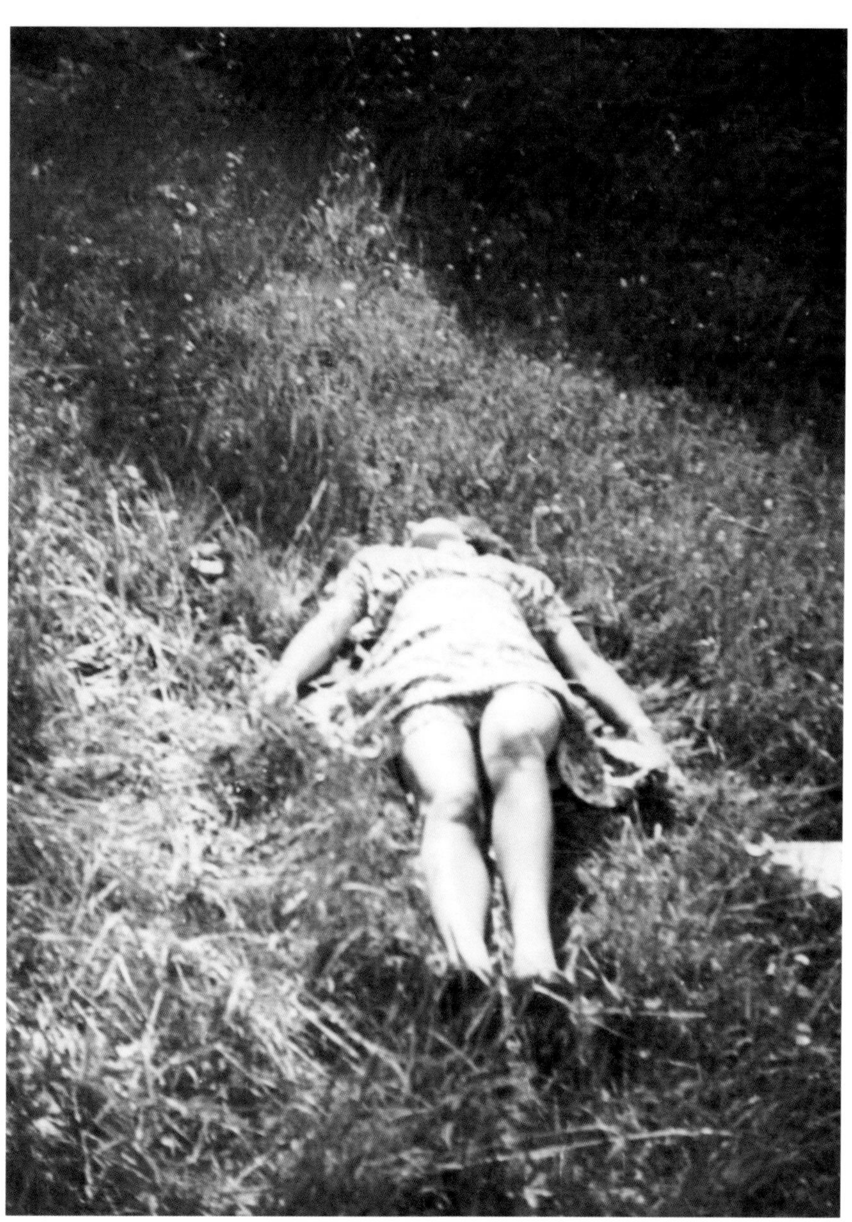

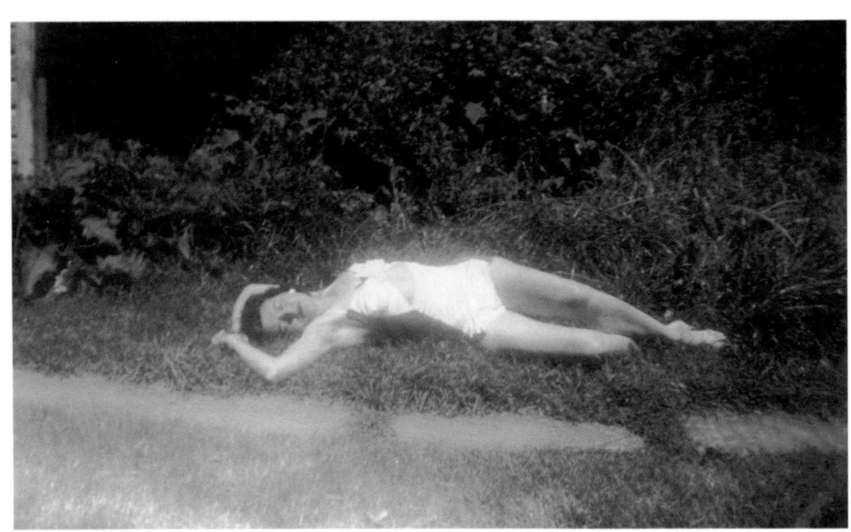

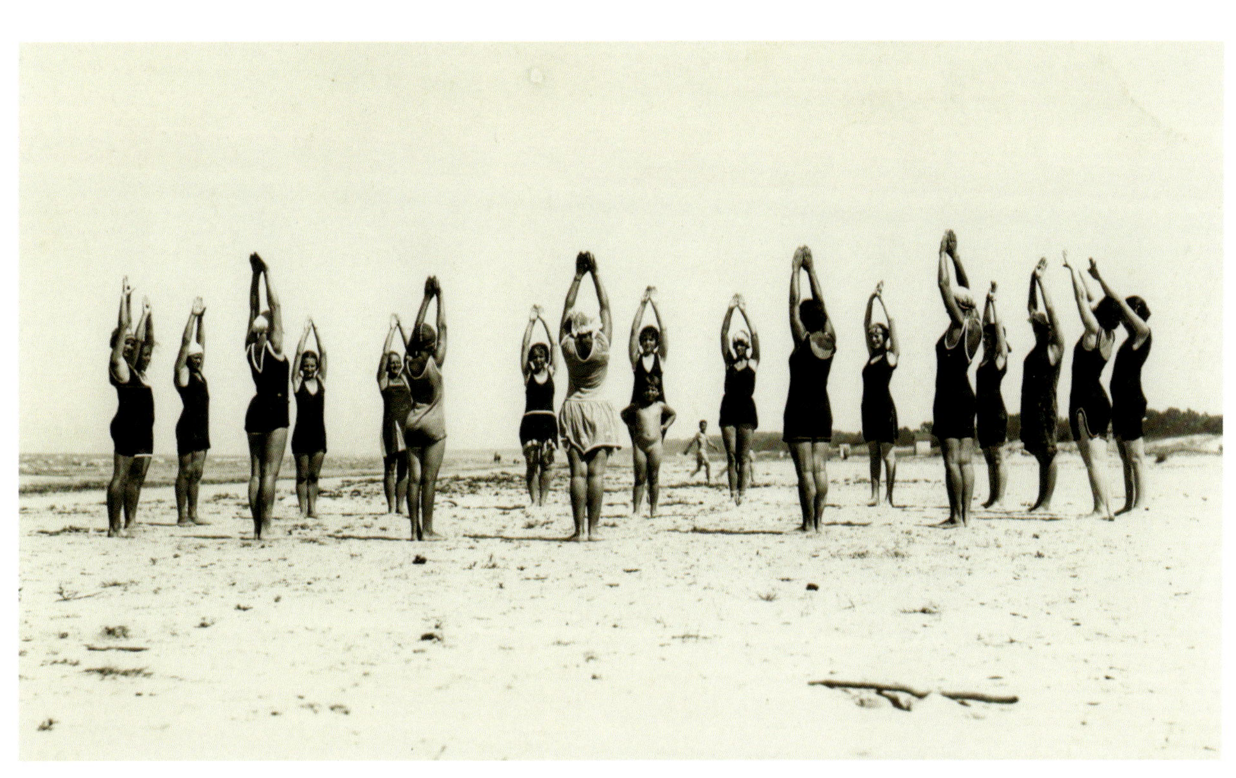

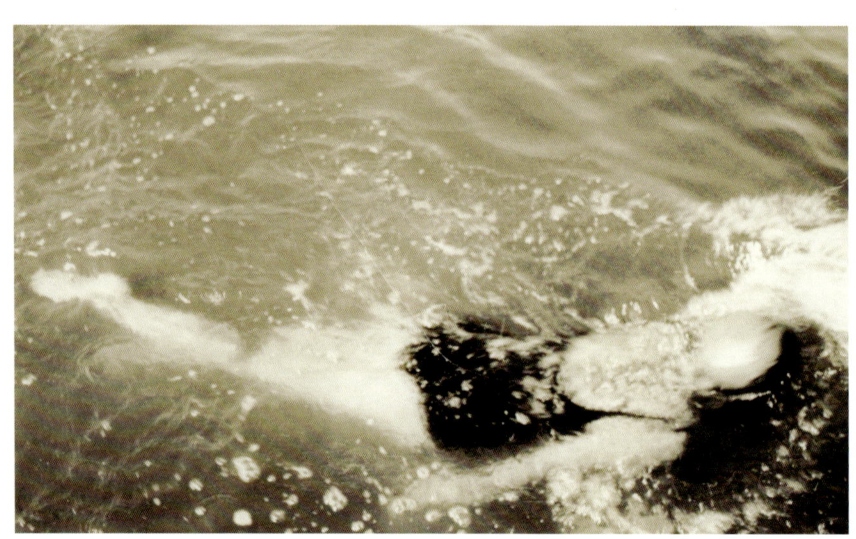

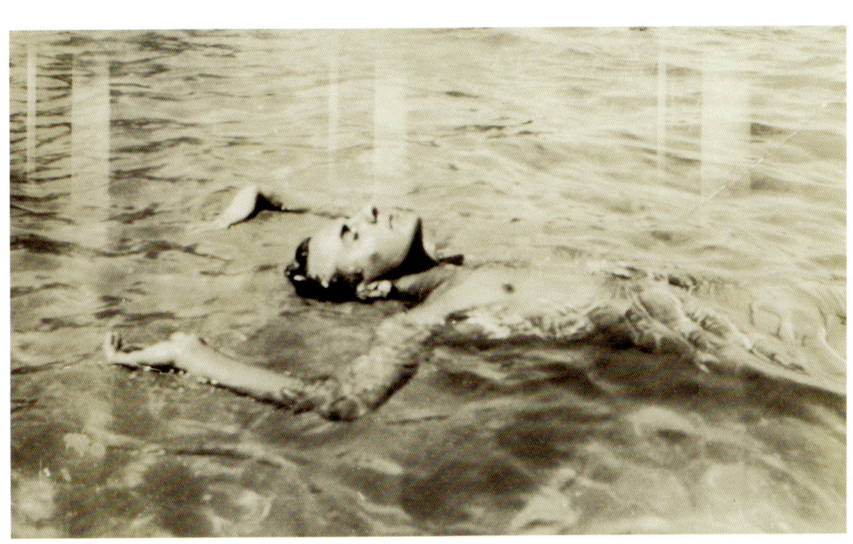

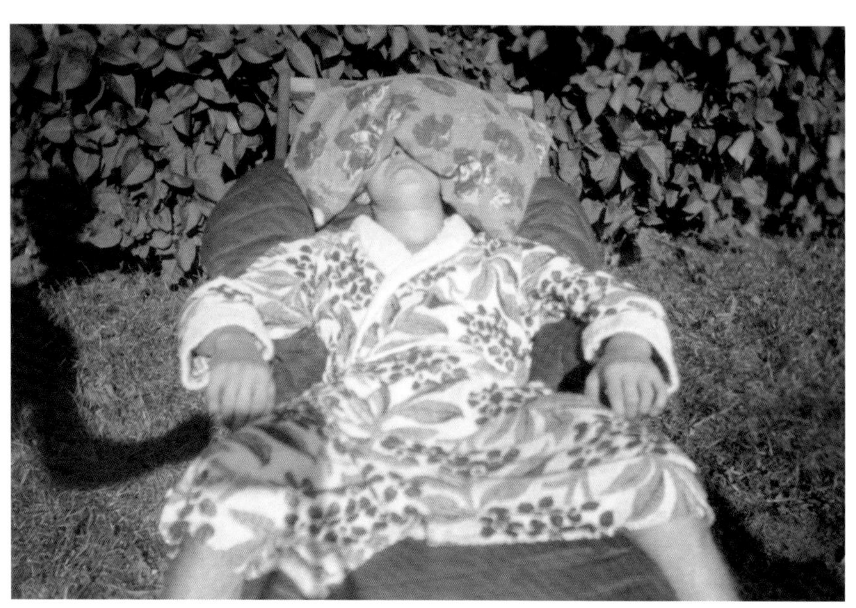

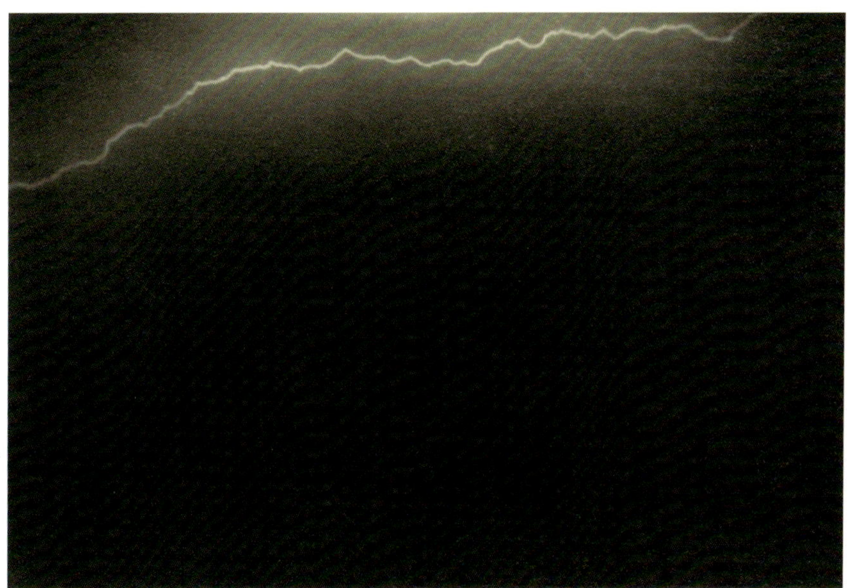

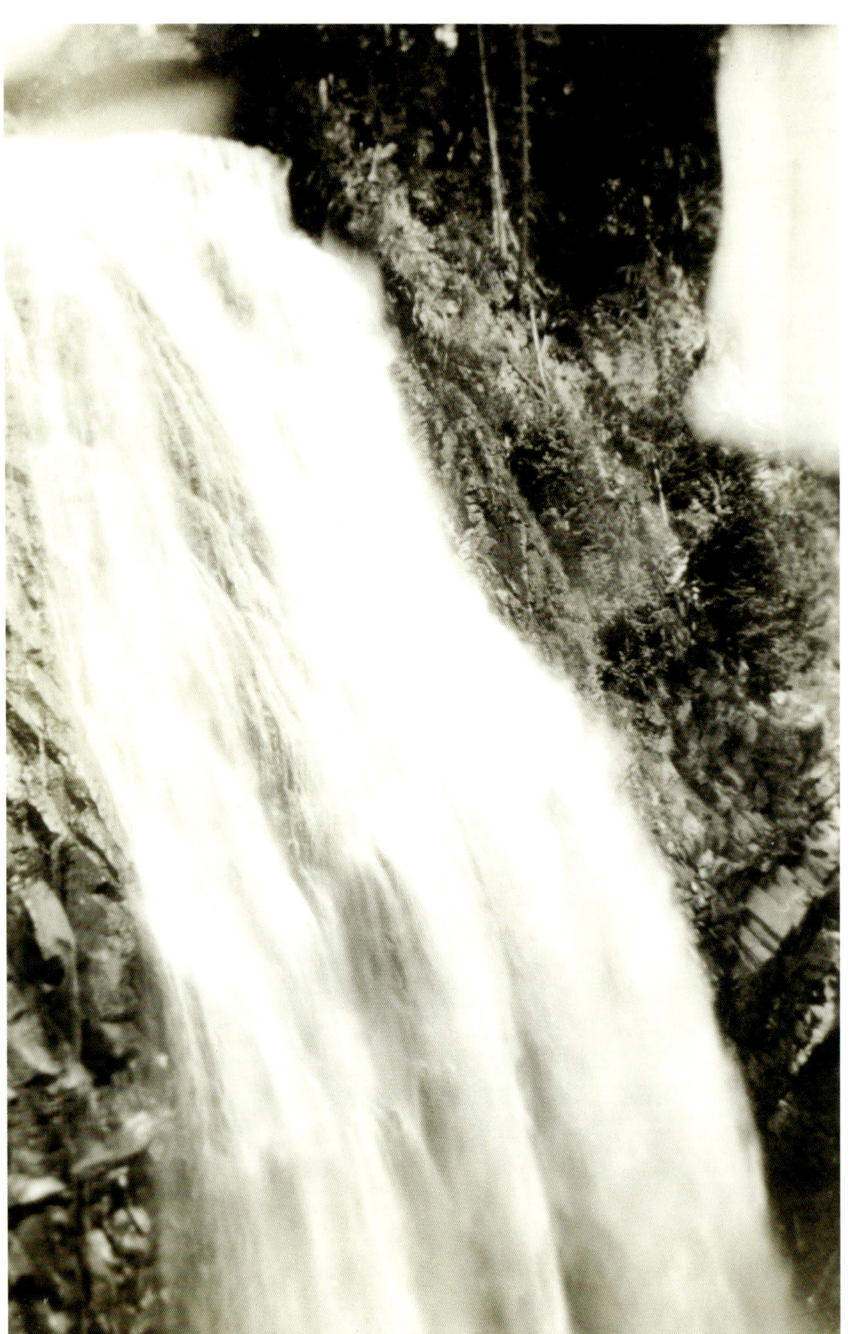

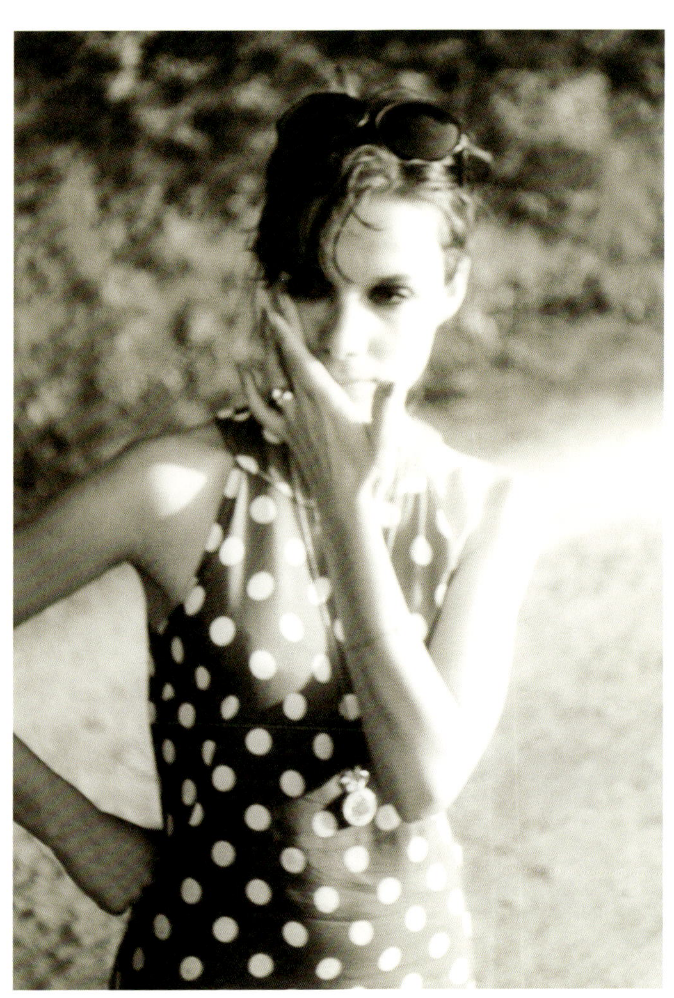

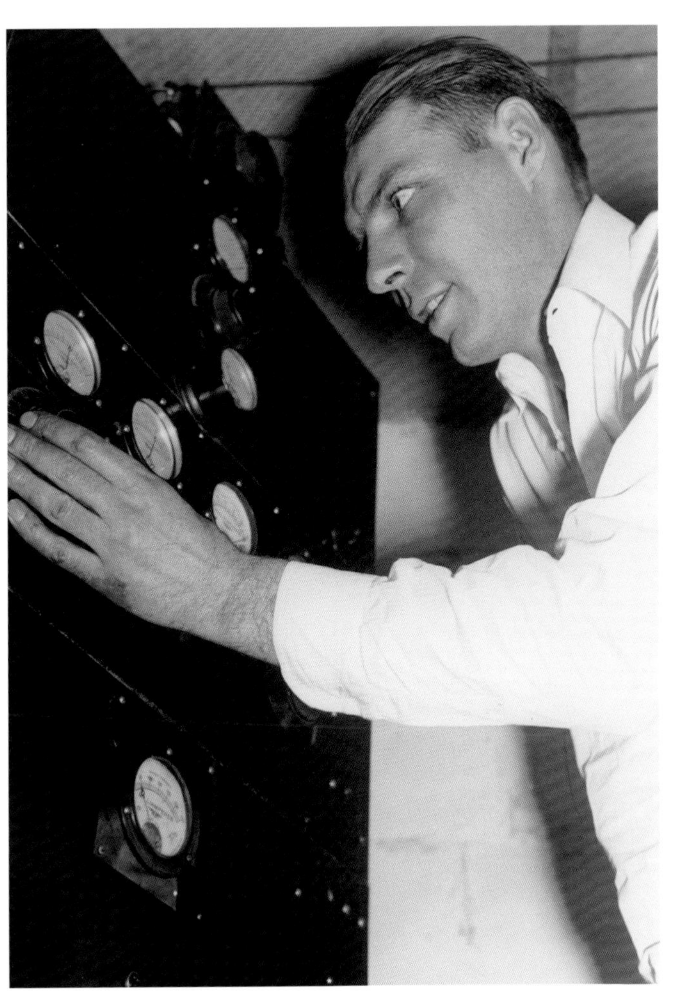

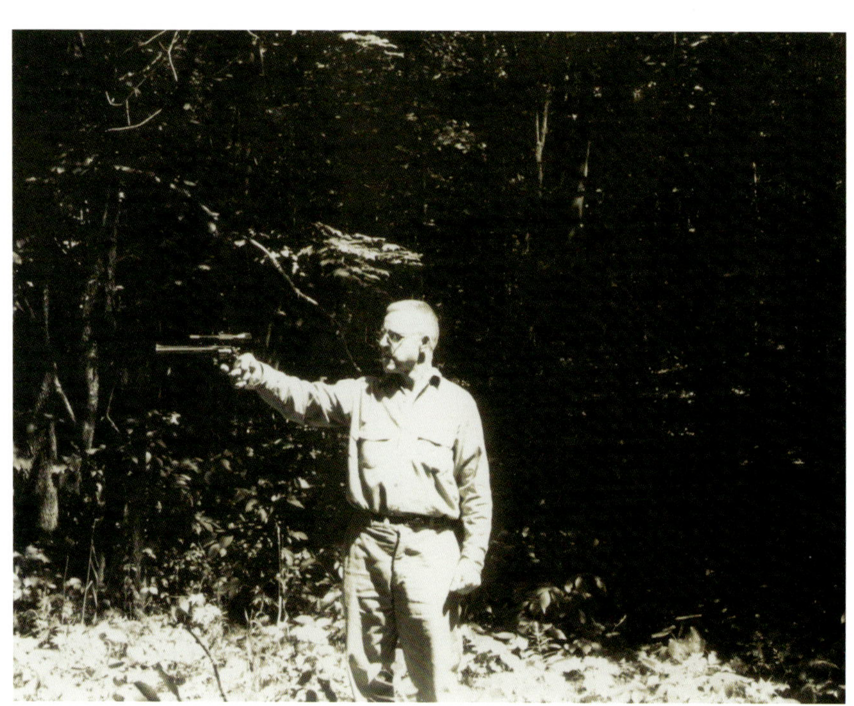

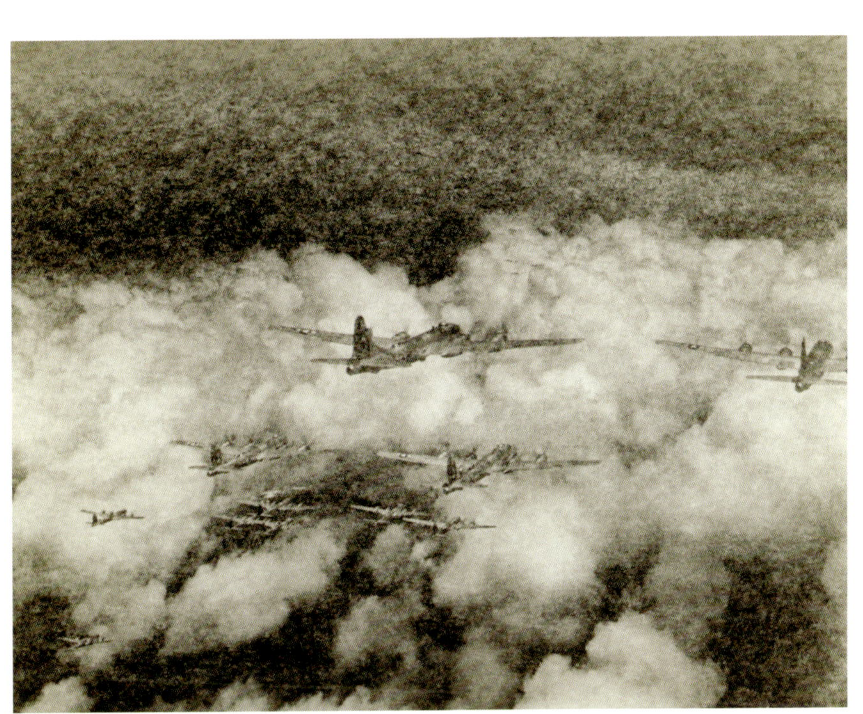

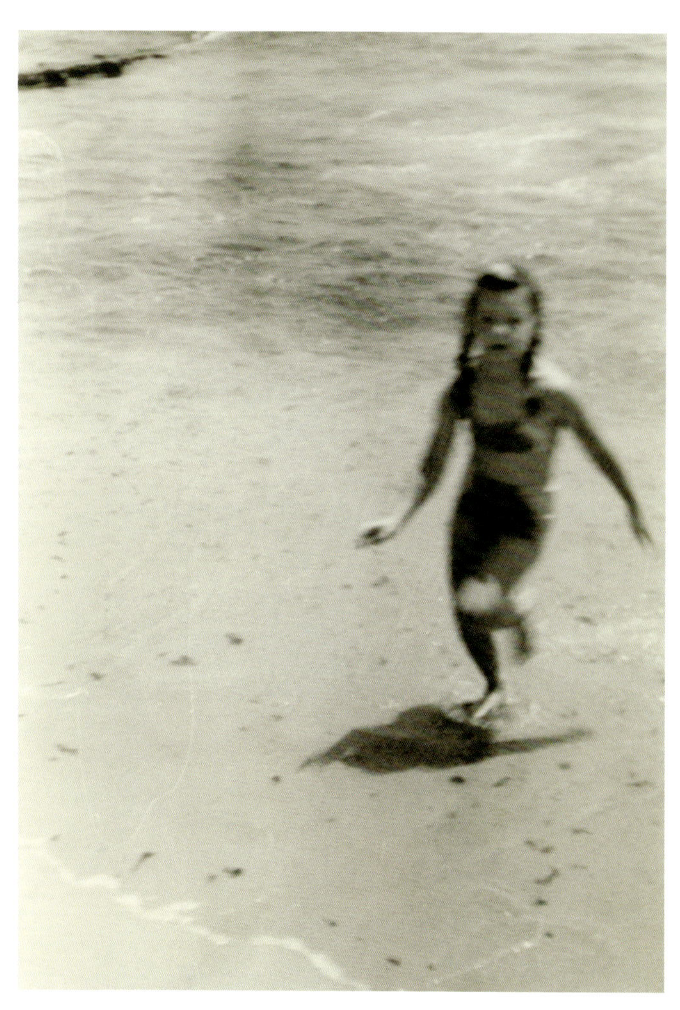

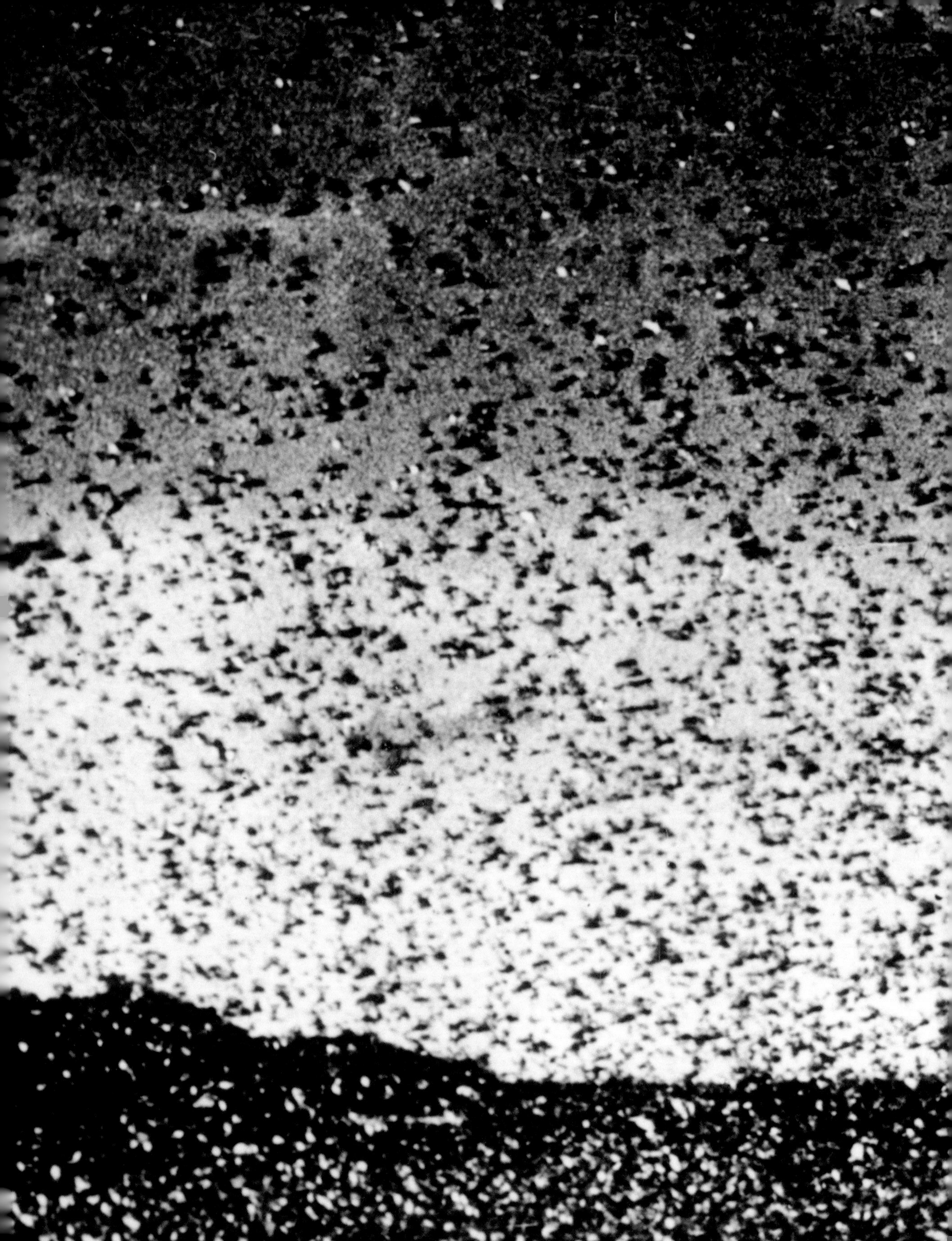

East Africa-Fall, 1943

A flight of the famous locusts of the Middle East. They practically darken the sky.

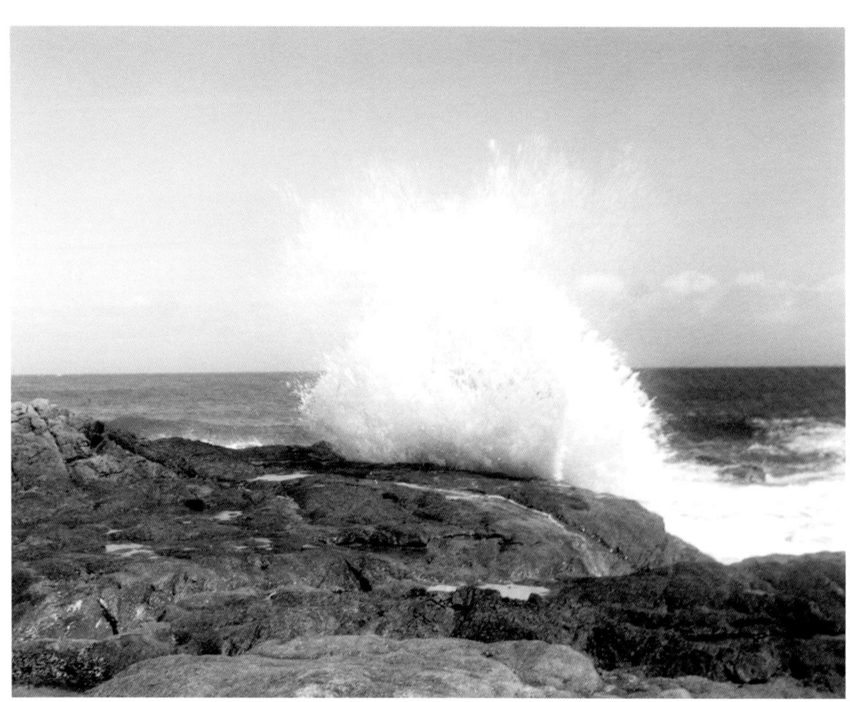

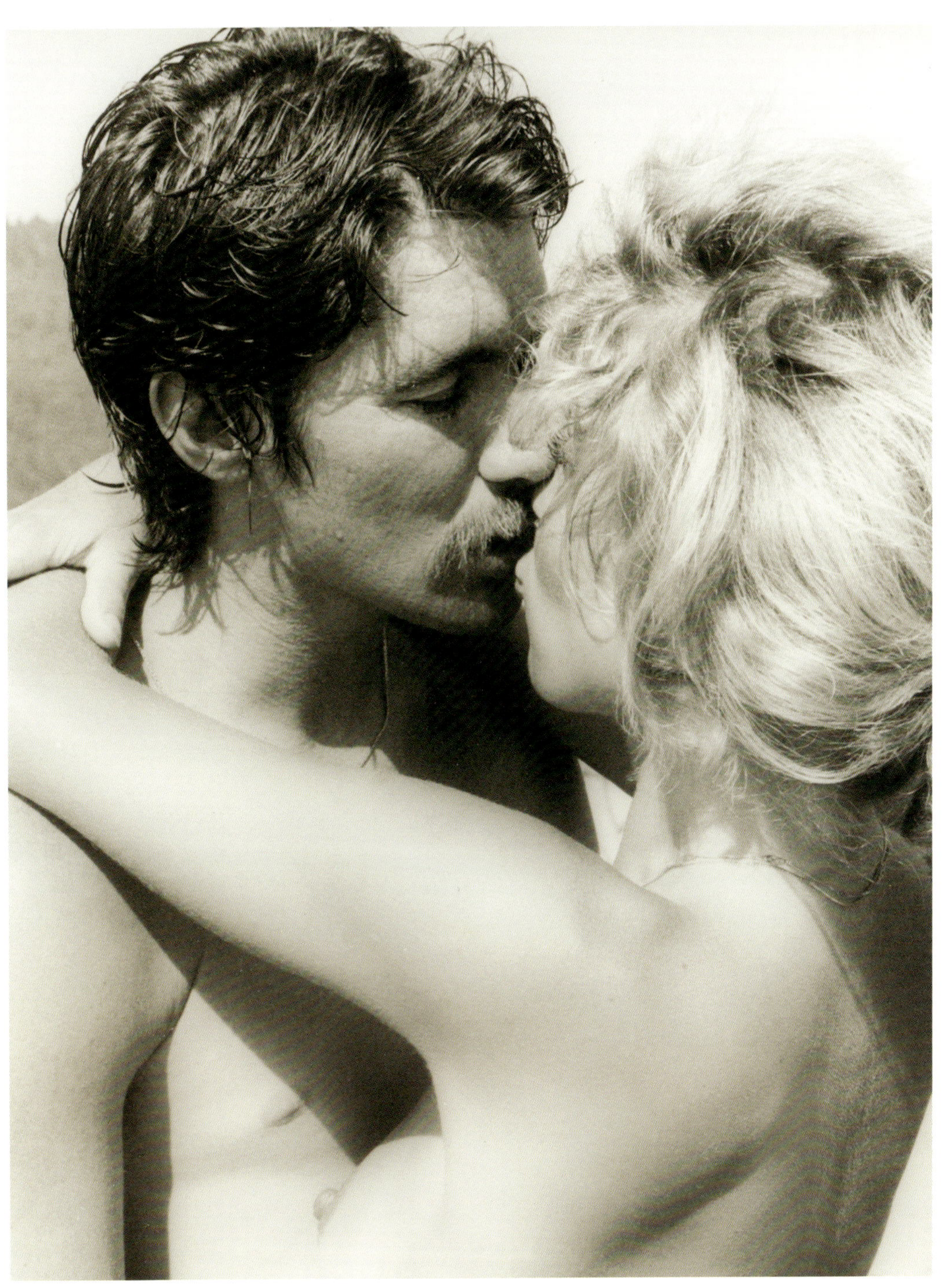

How the Isl
6 miles ou
the night

ER C.1935 55 2002

nd look from
l at sea in

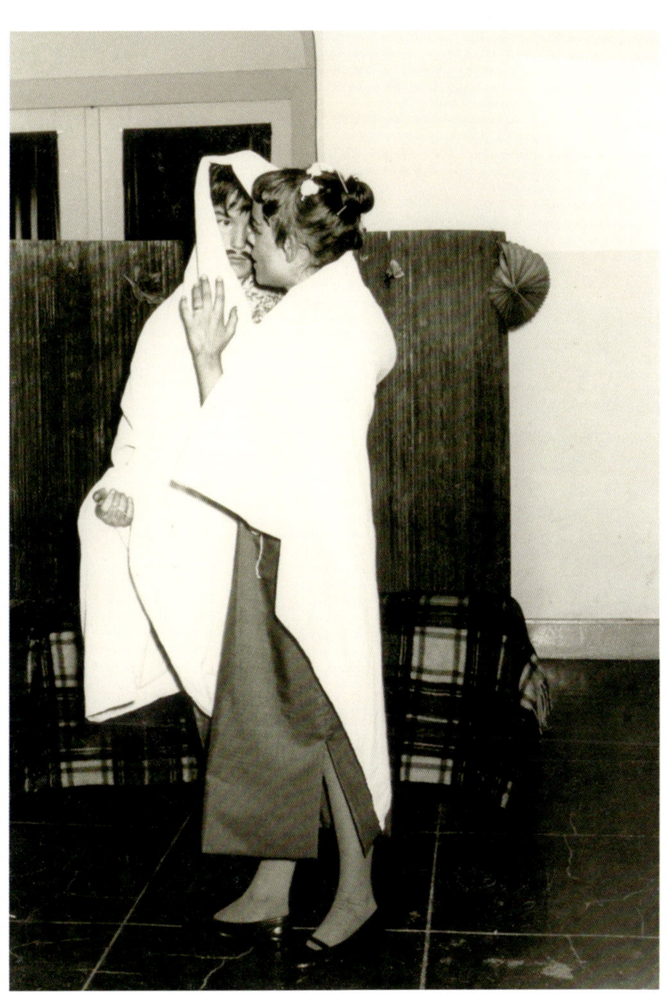

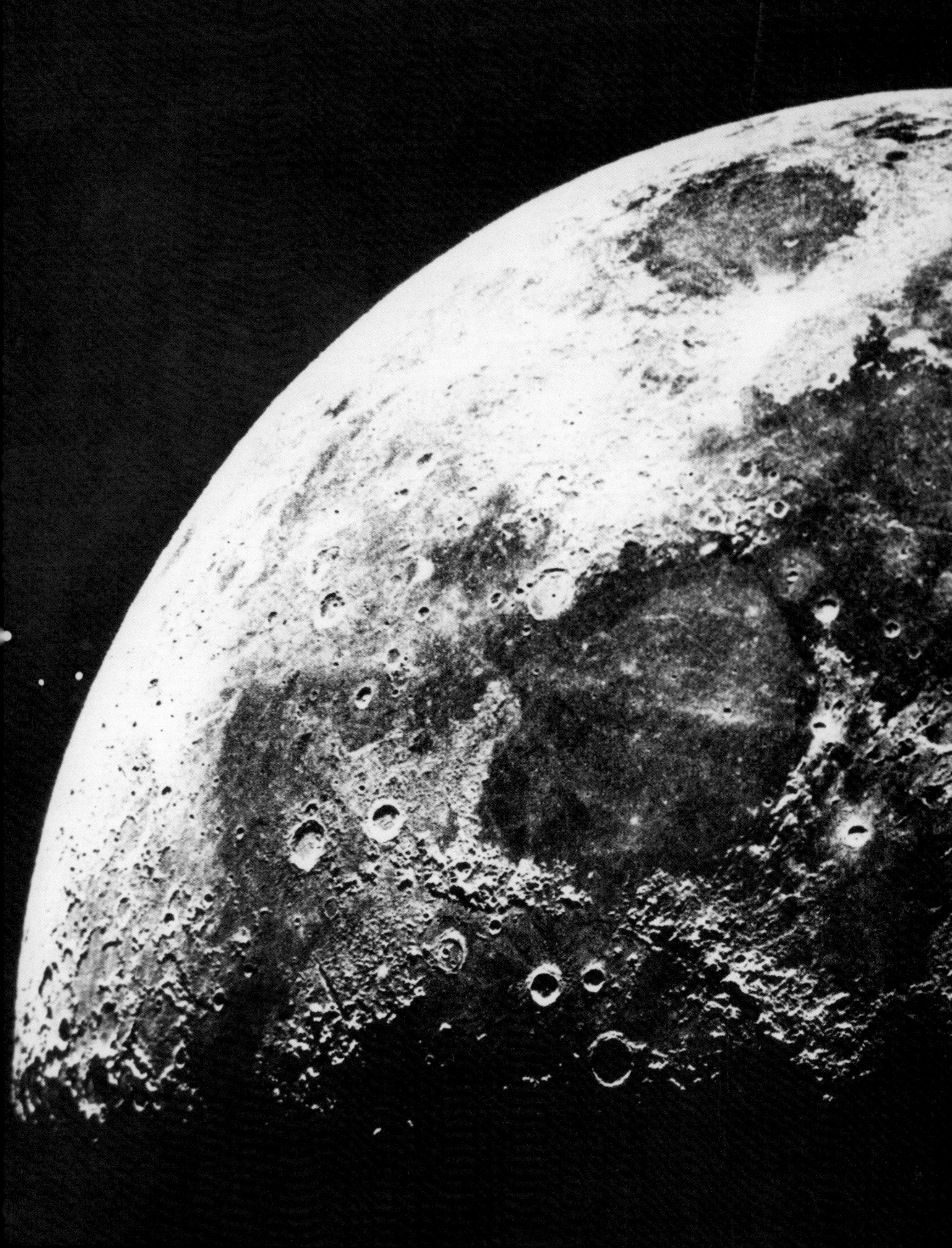

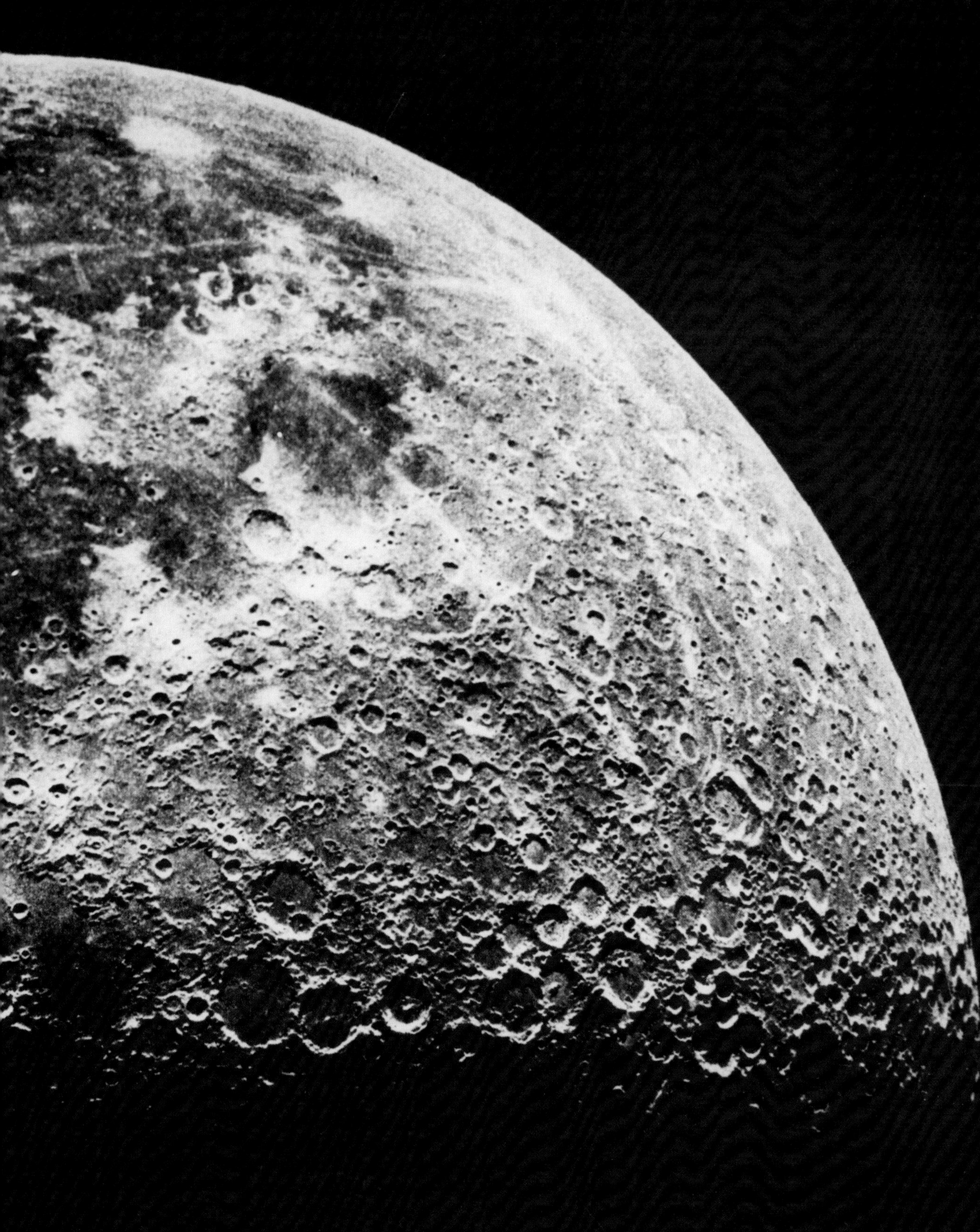

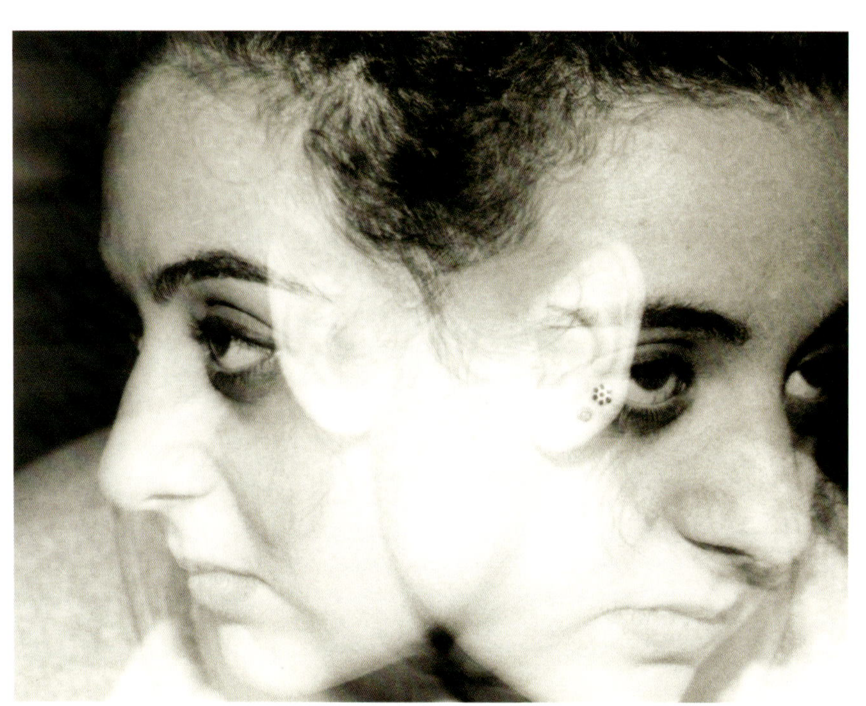

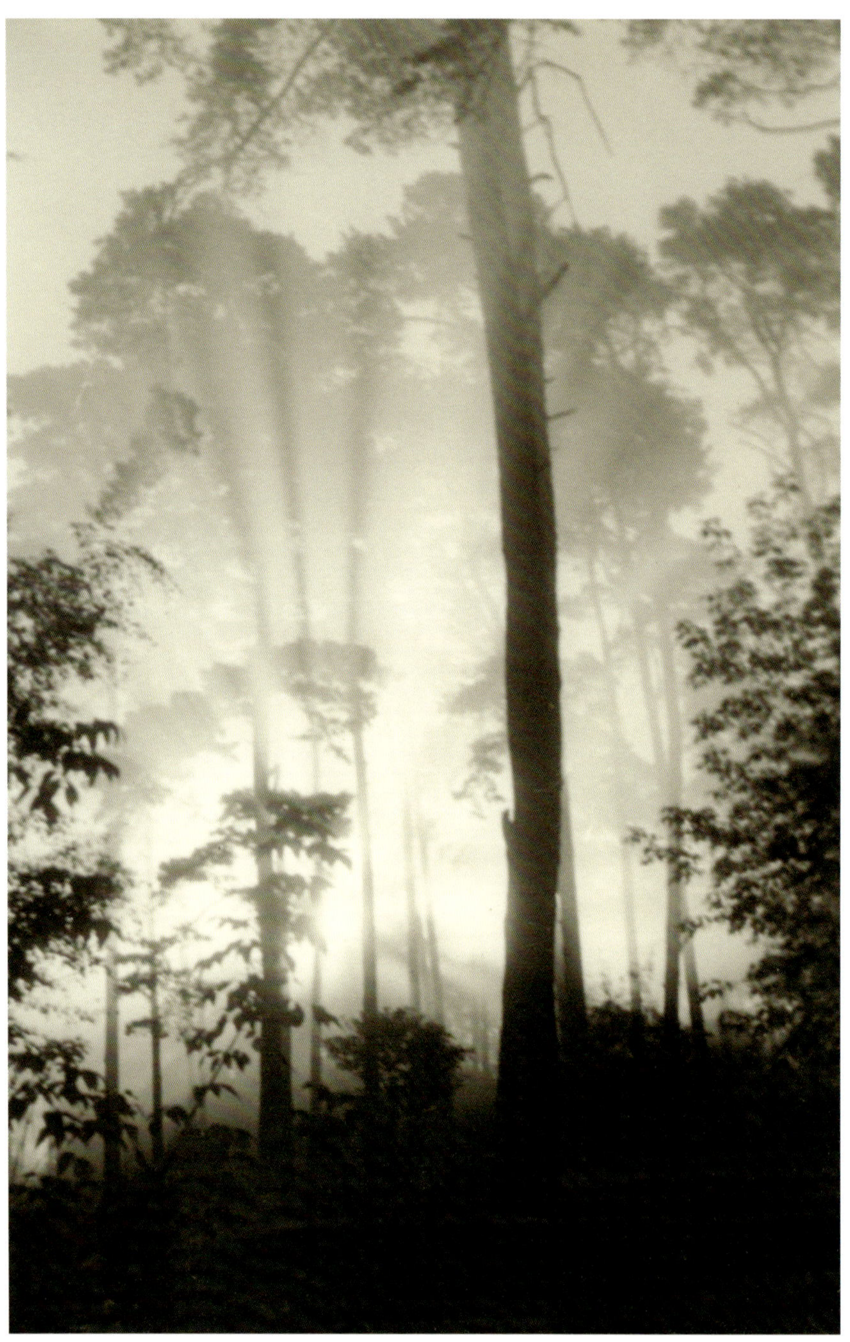

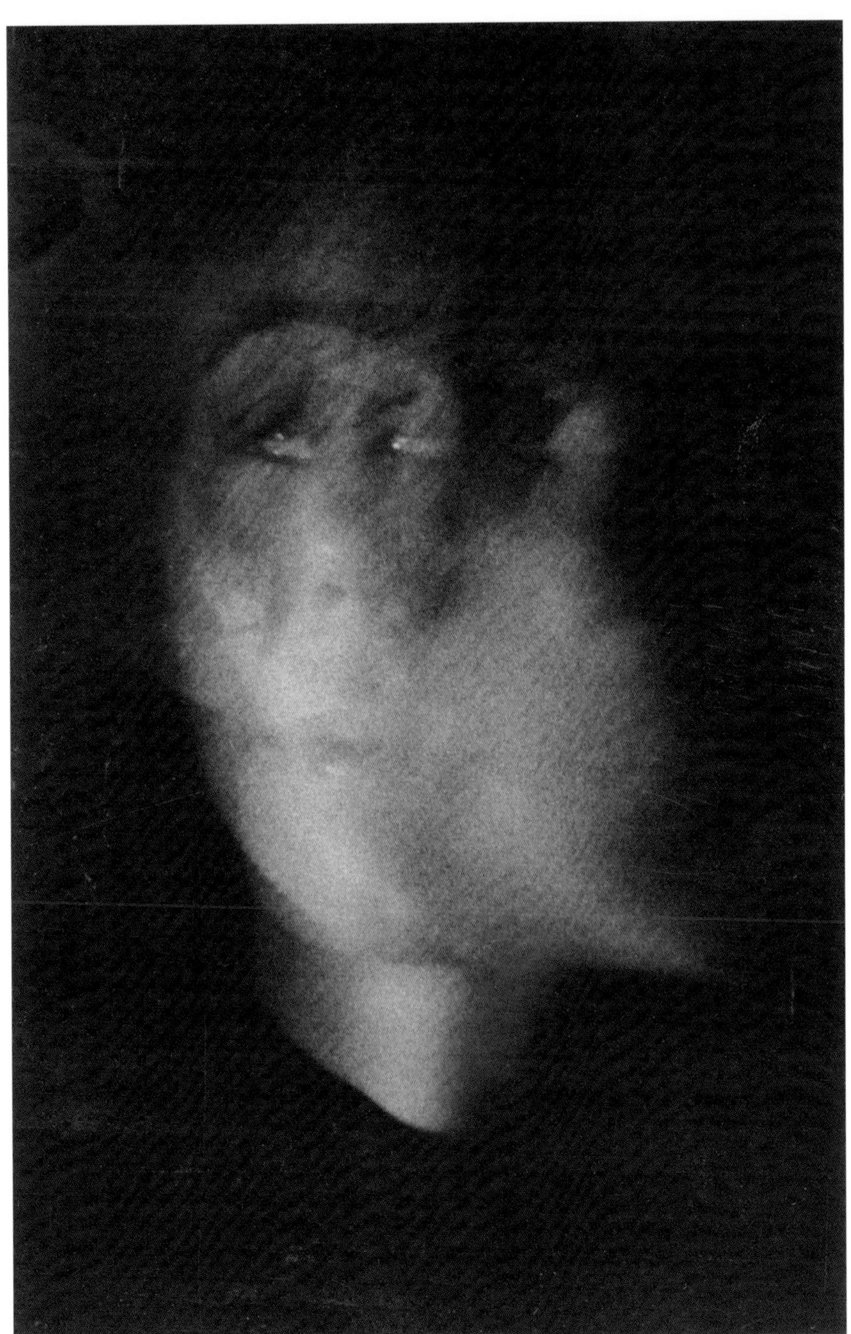

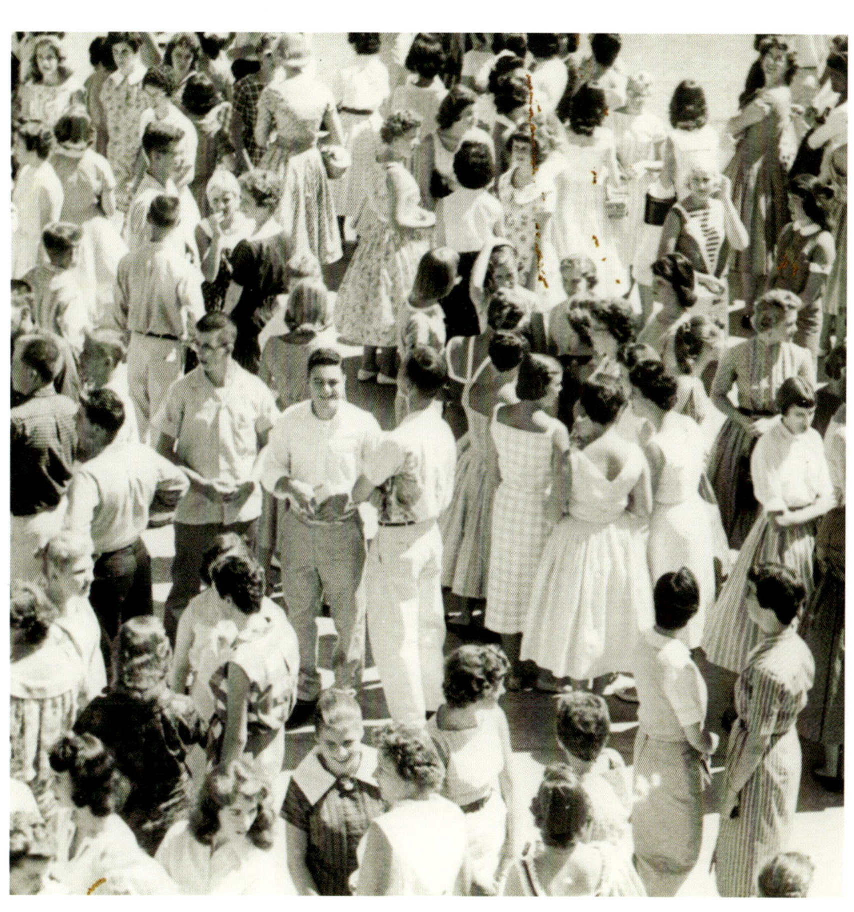

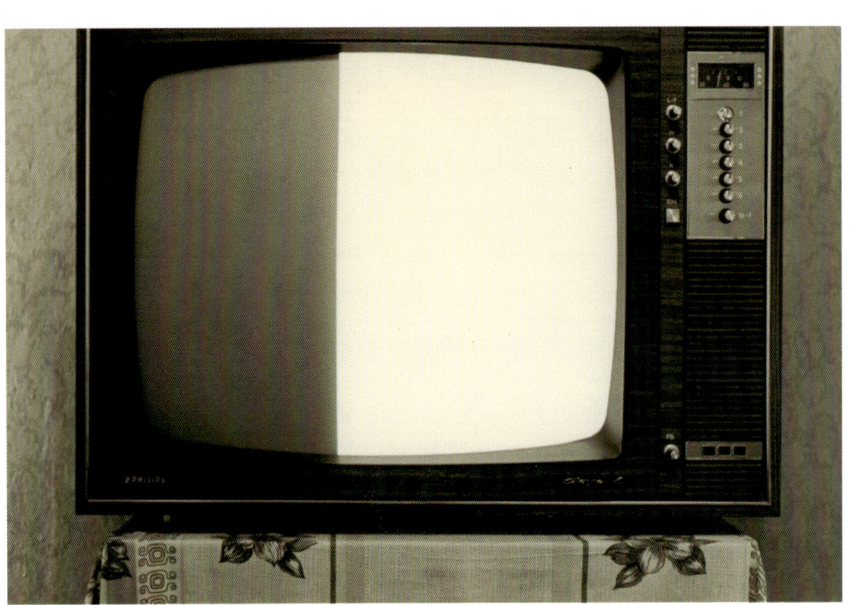
PHILIPS

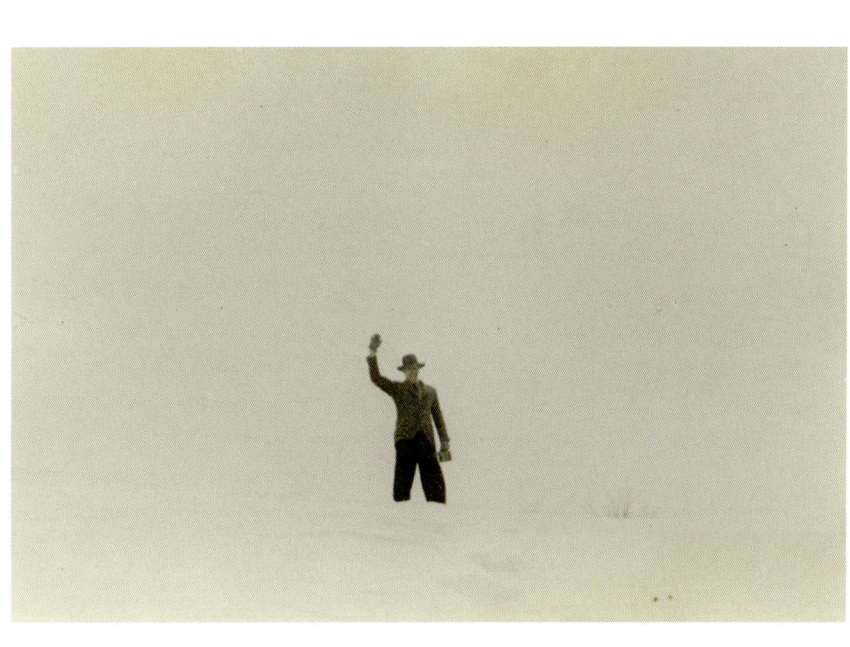

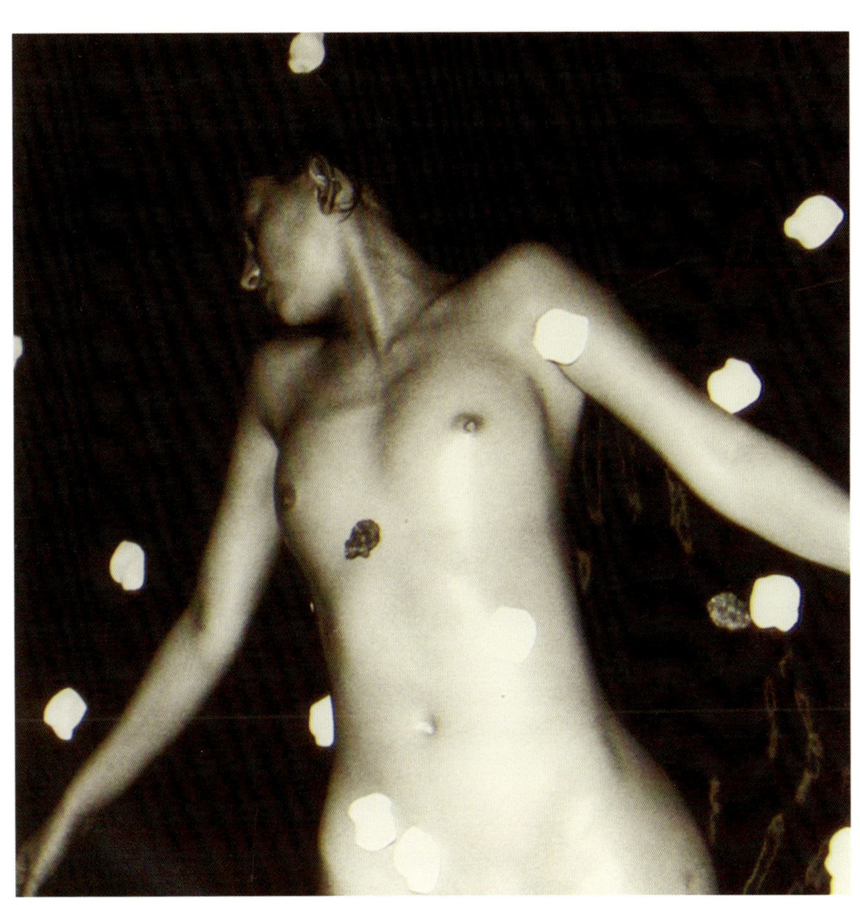

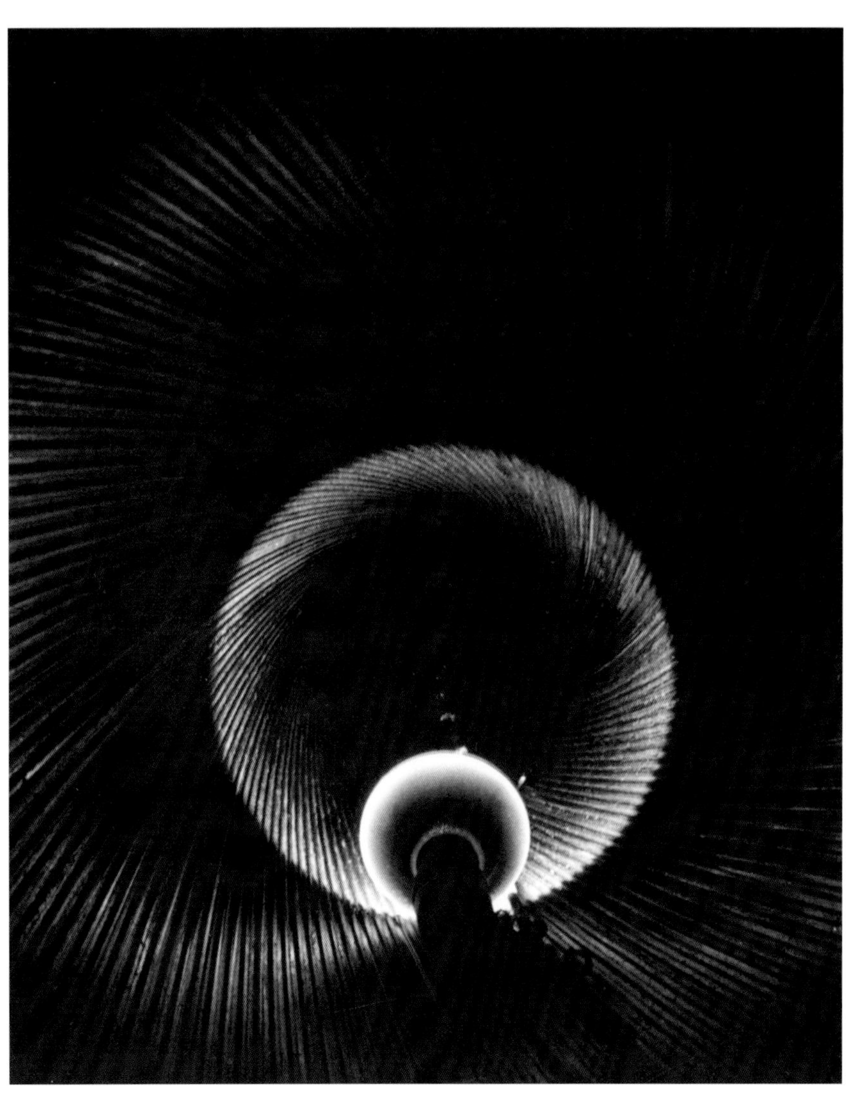

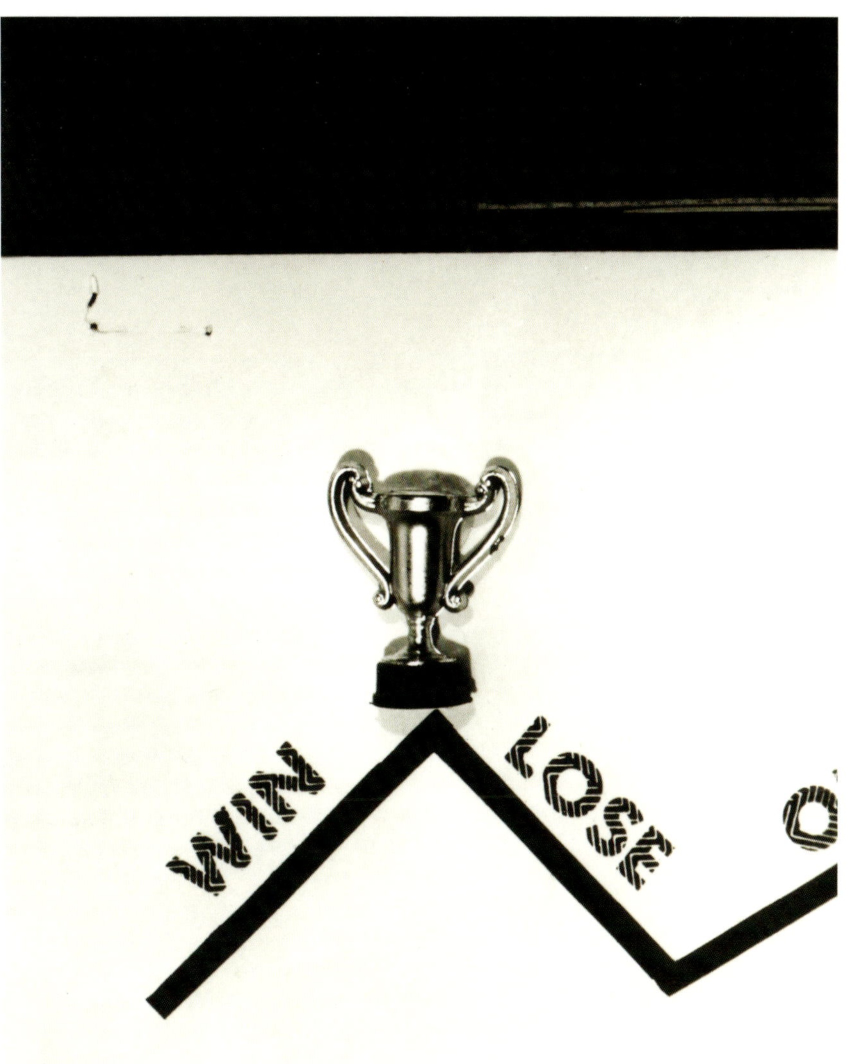
WIN
LOSE

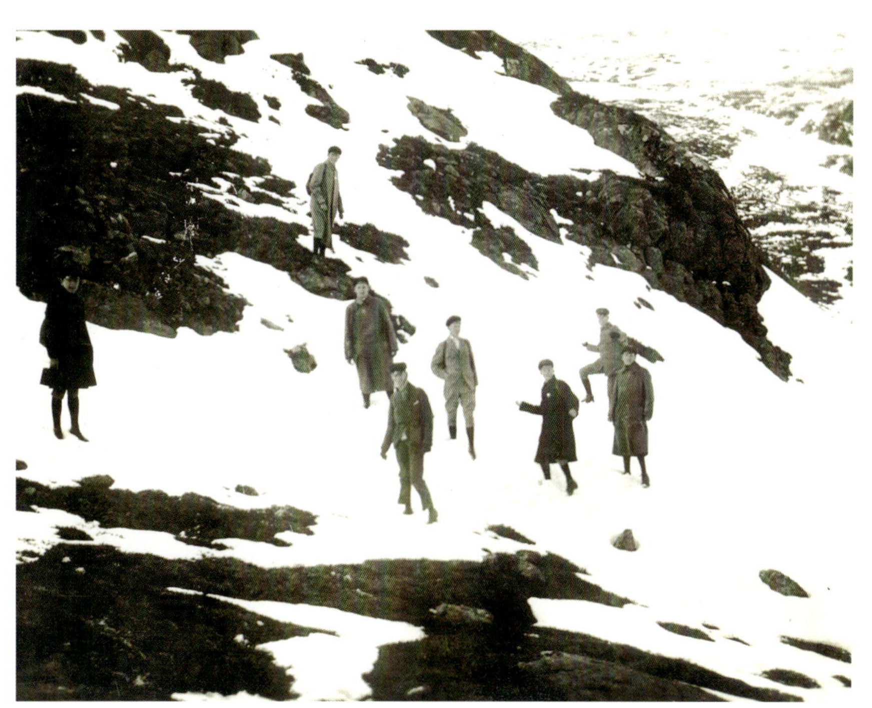

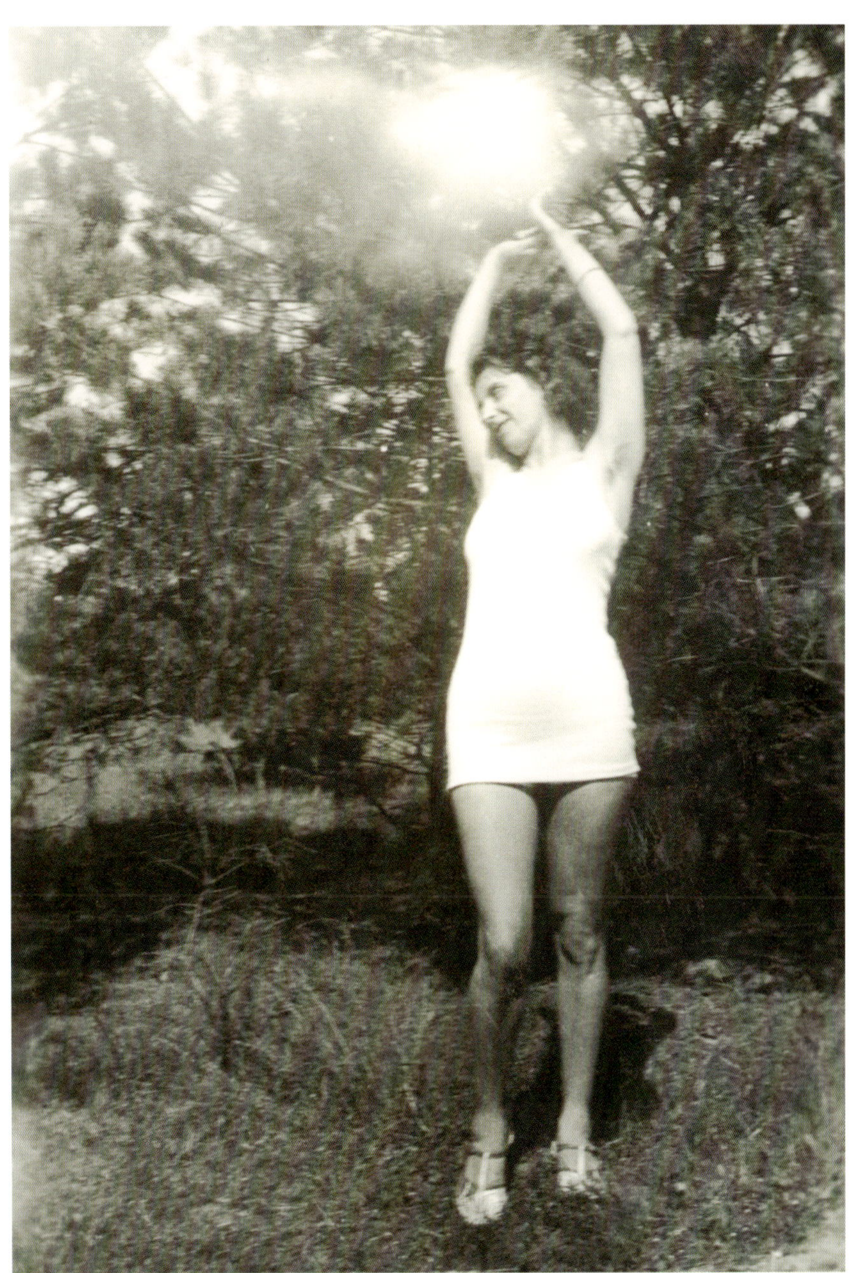

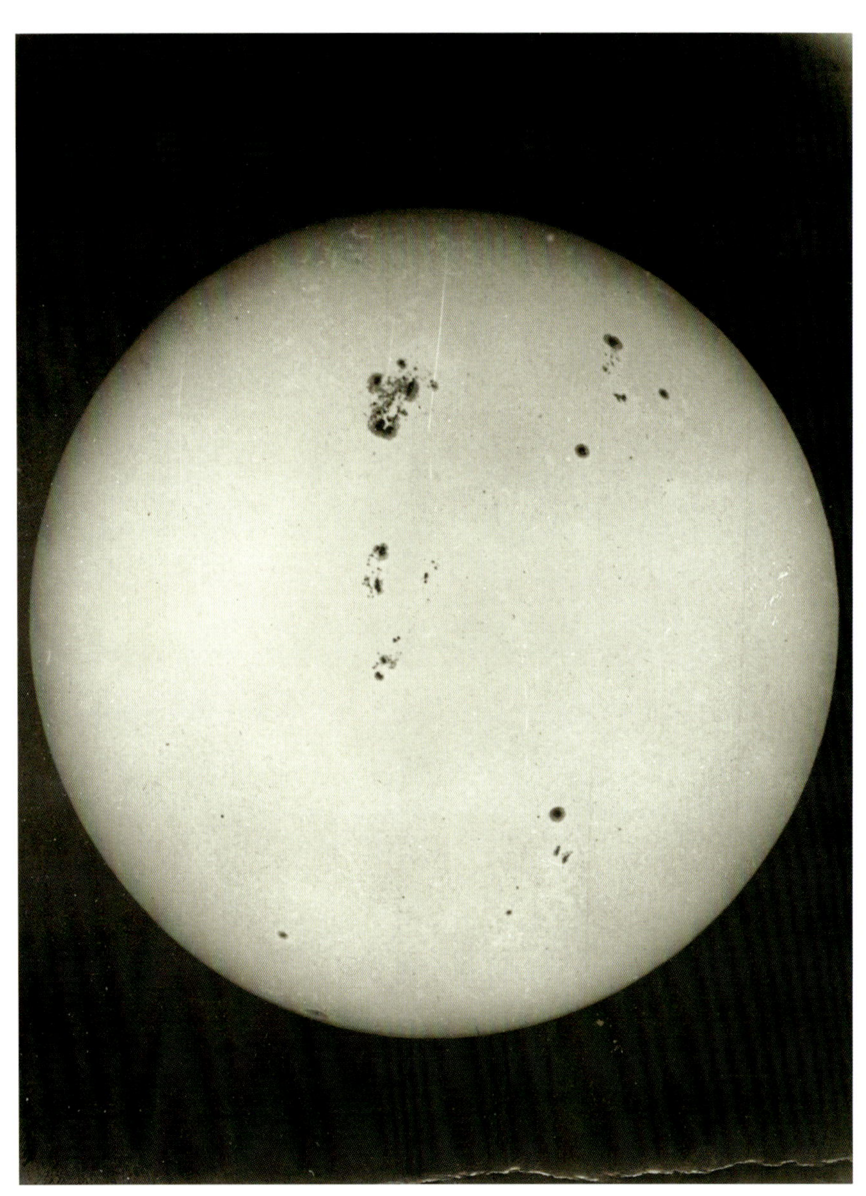

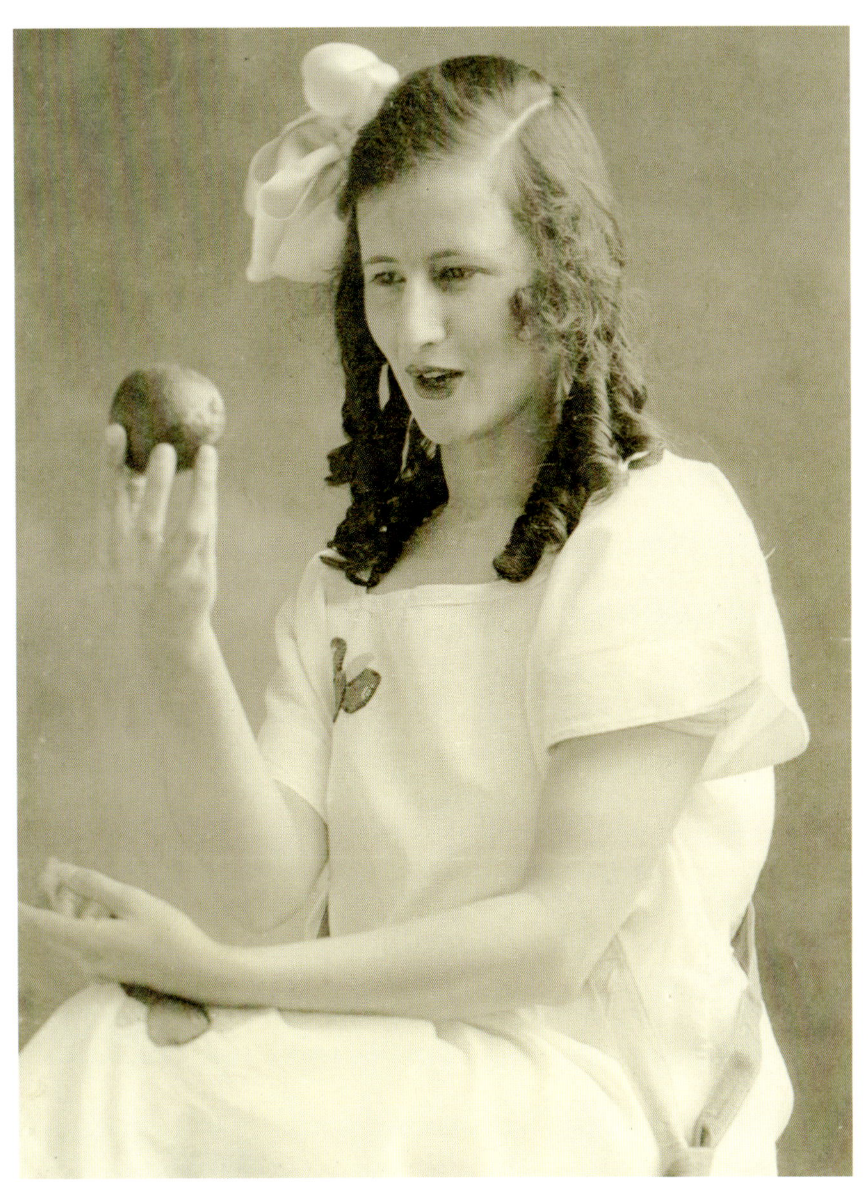

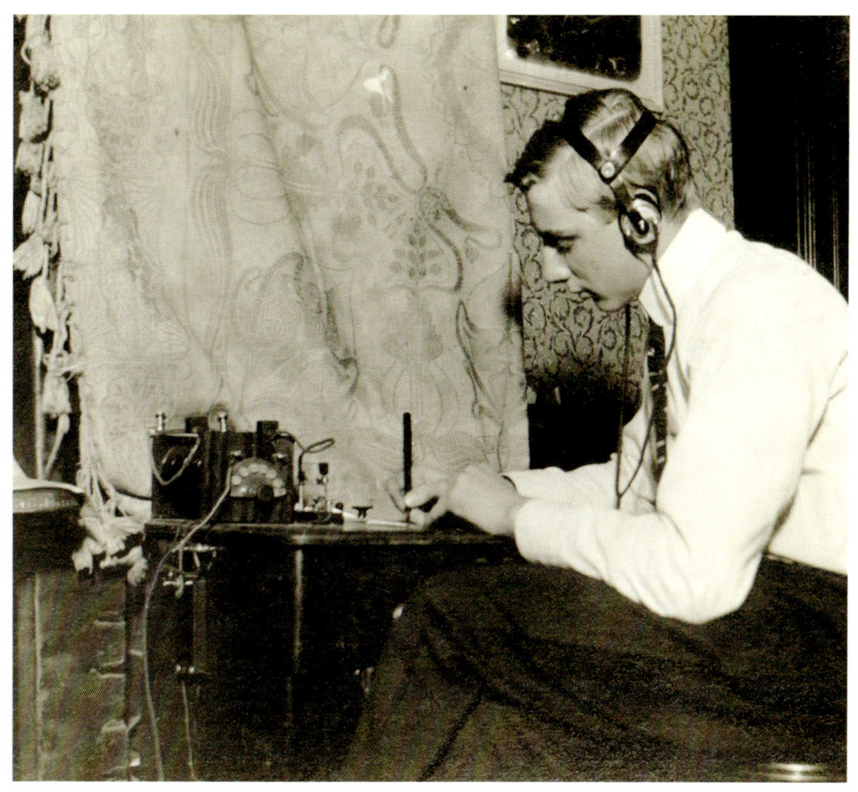

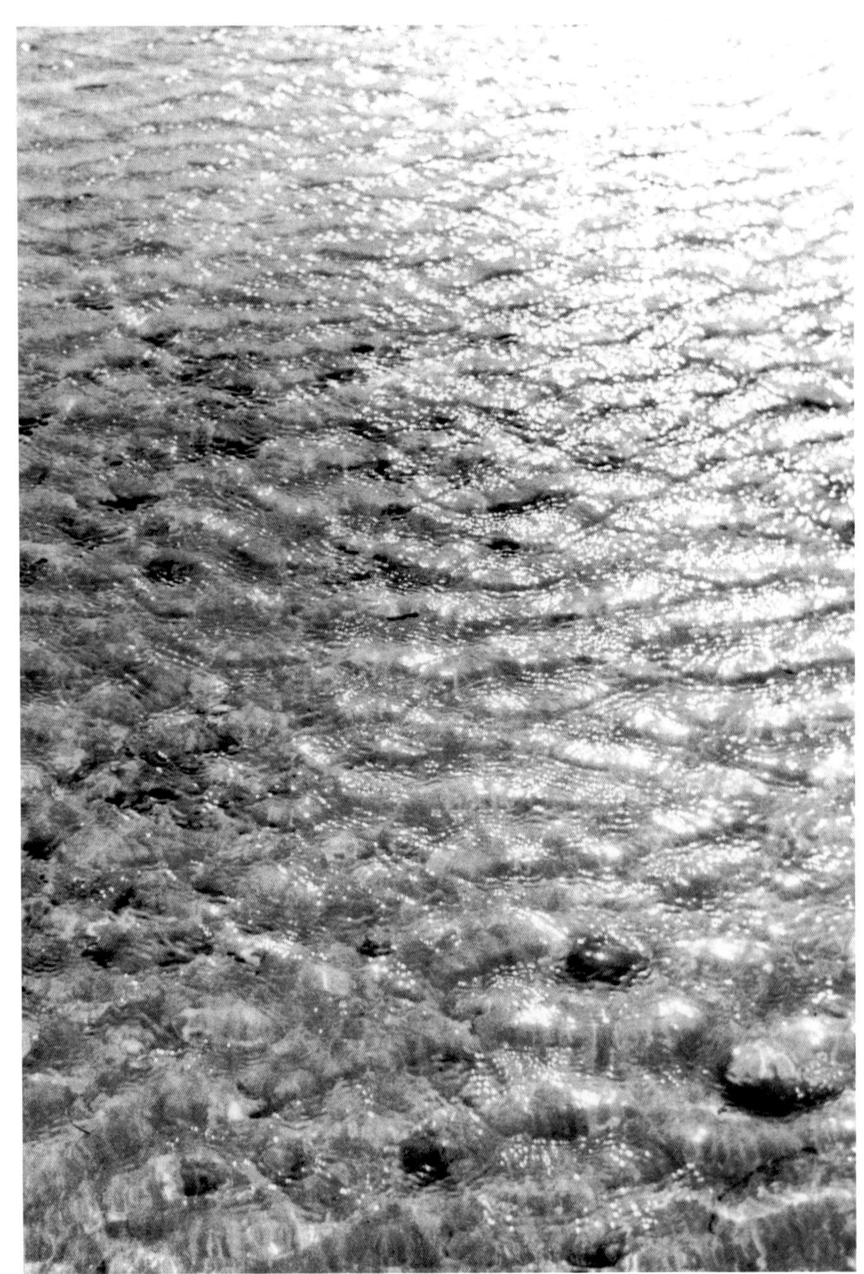

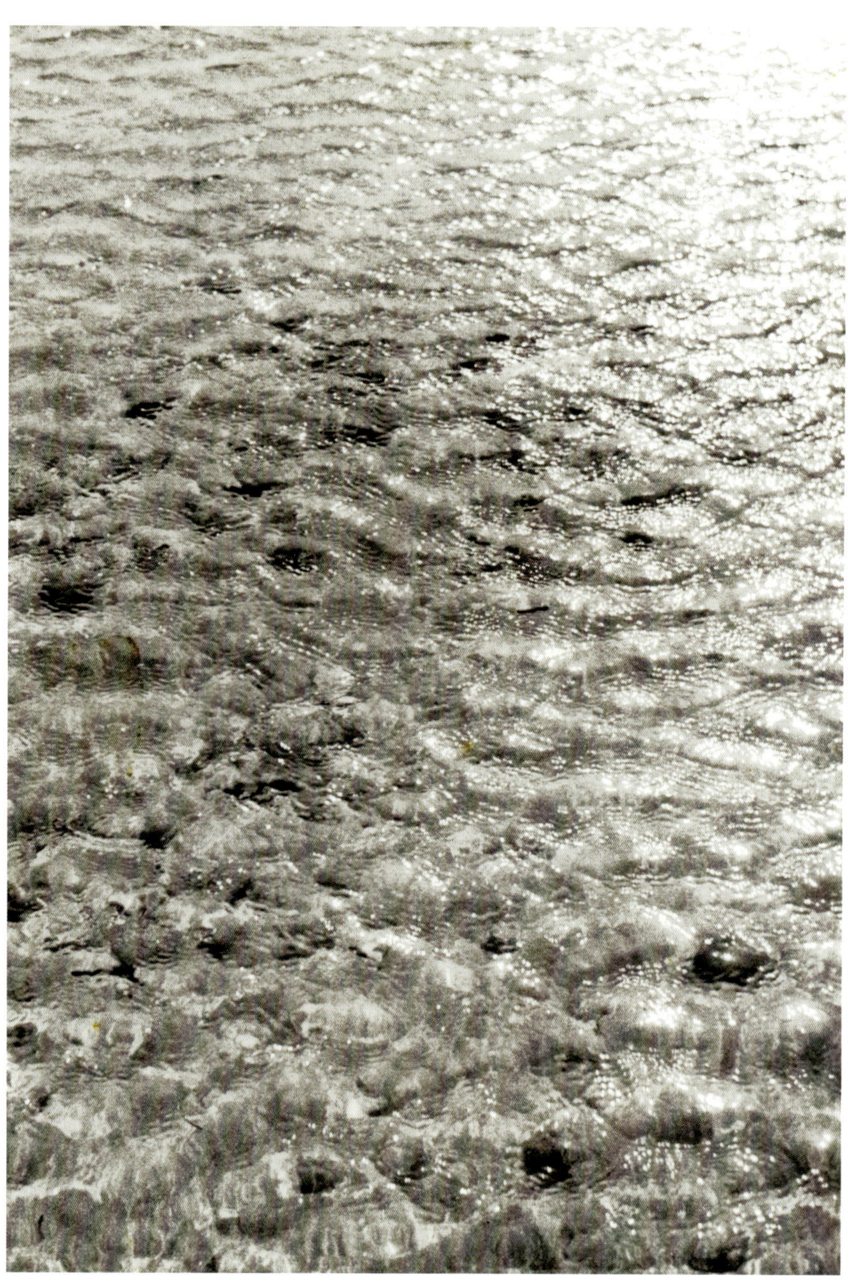

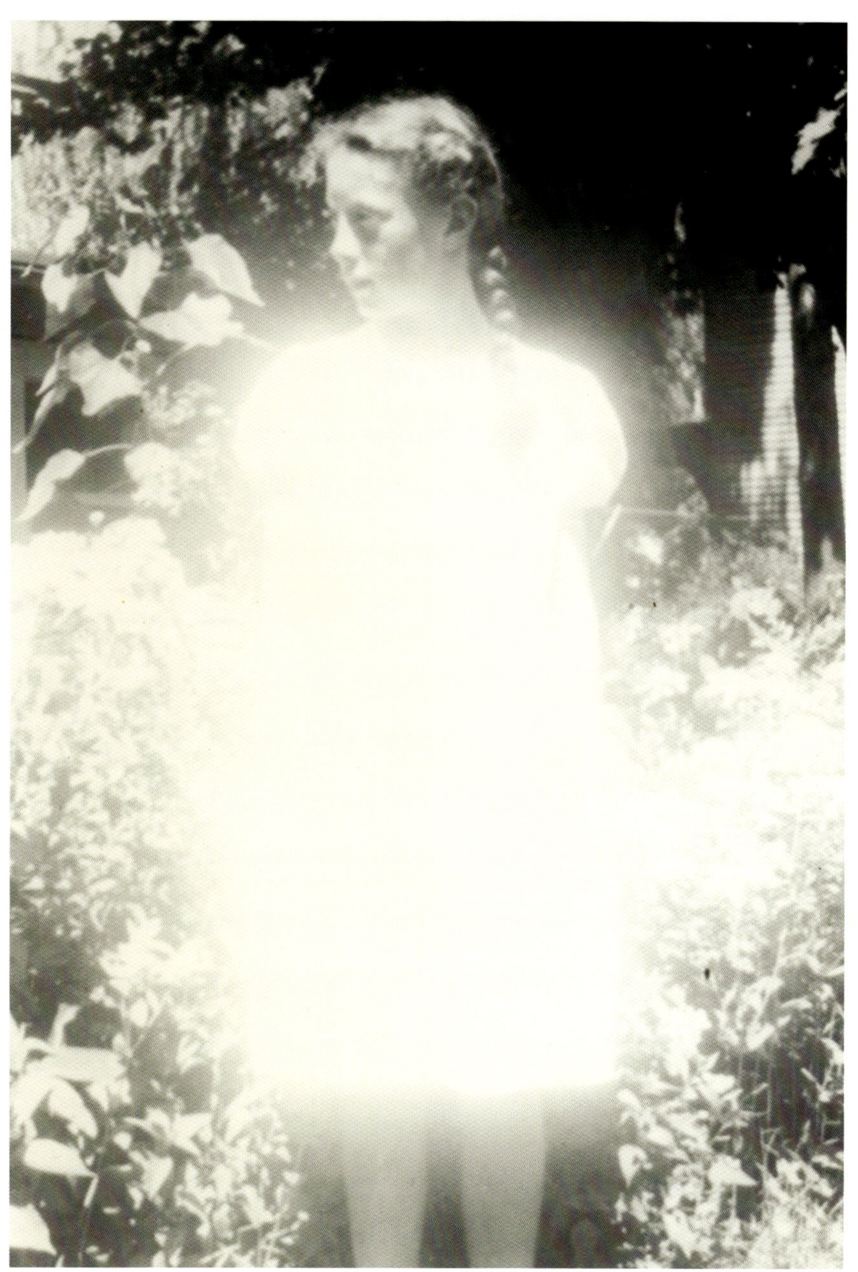

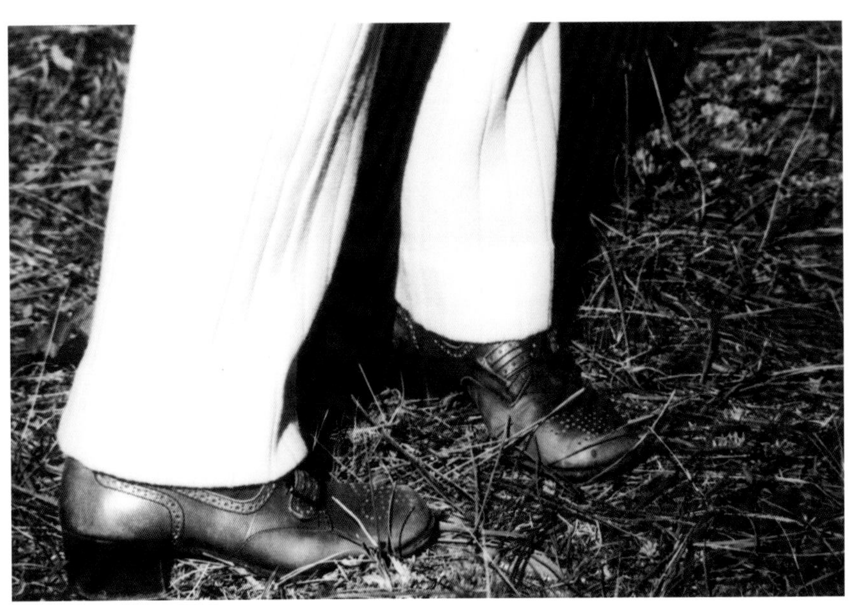

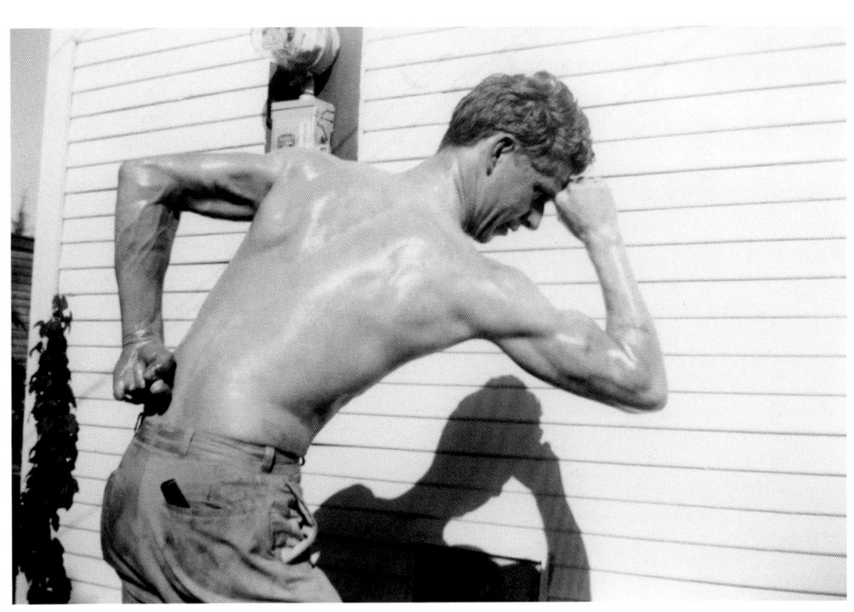

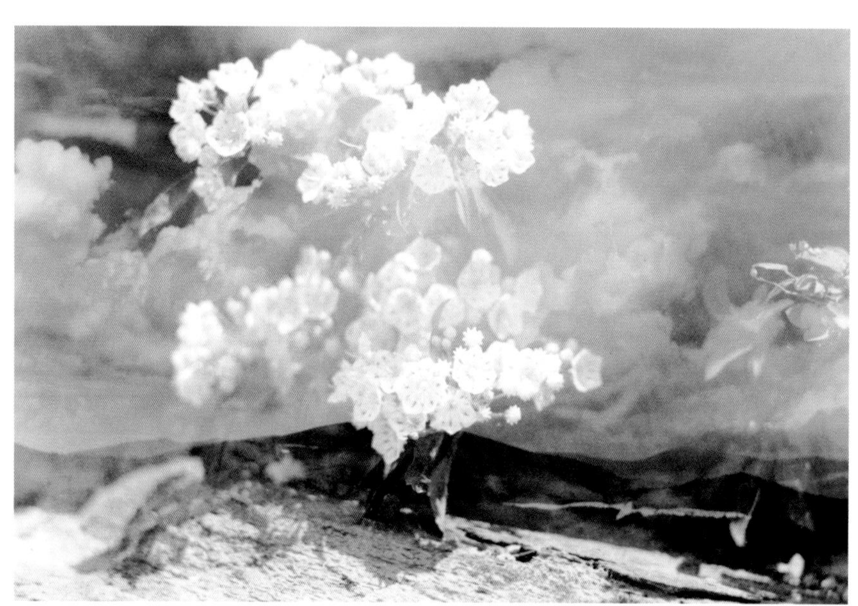

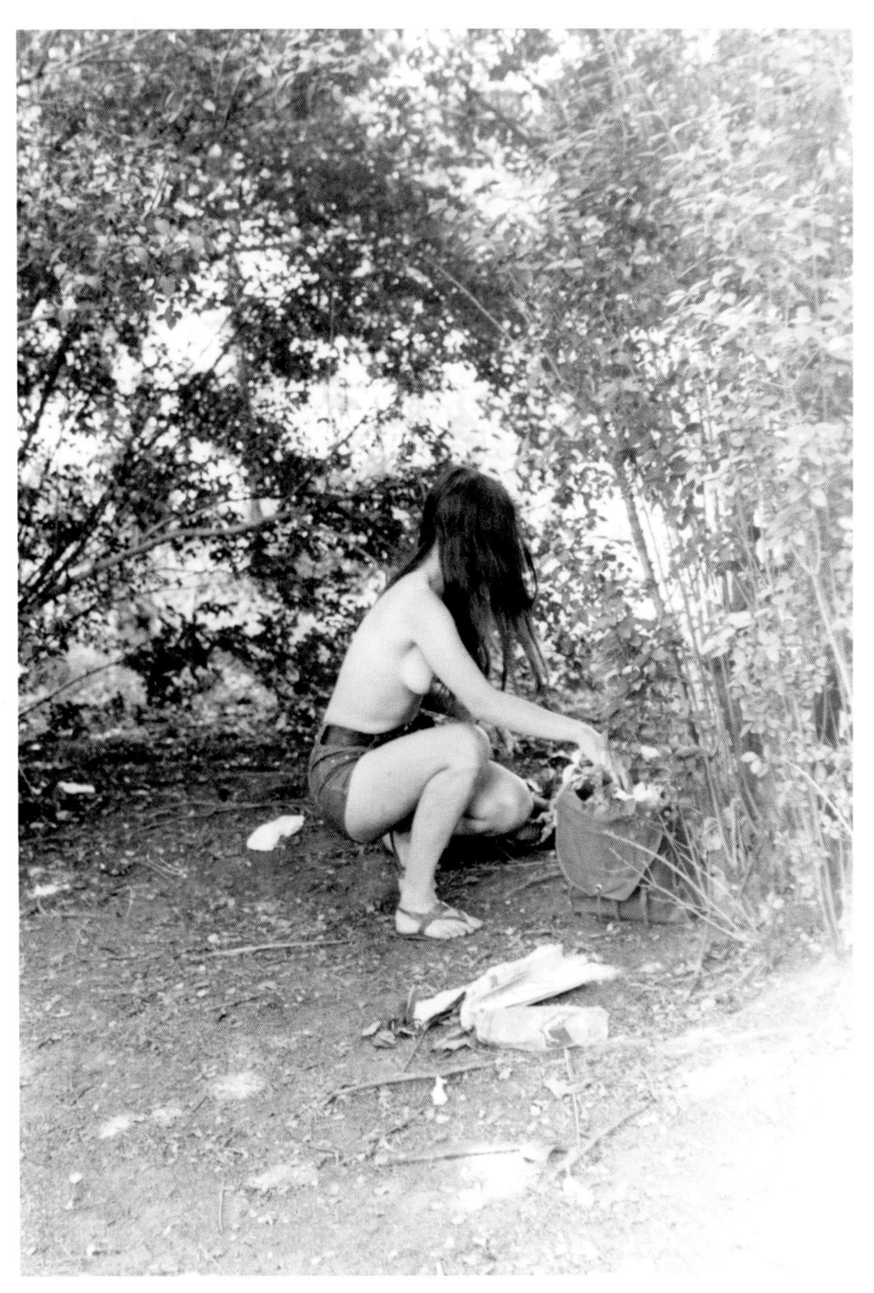

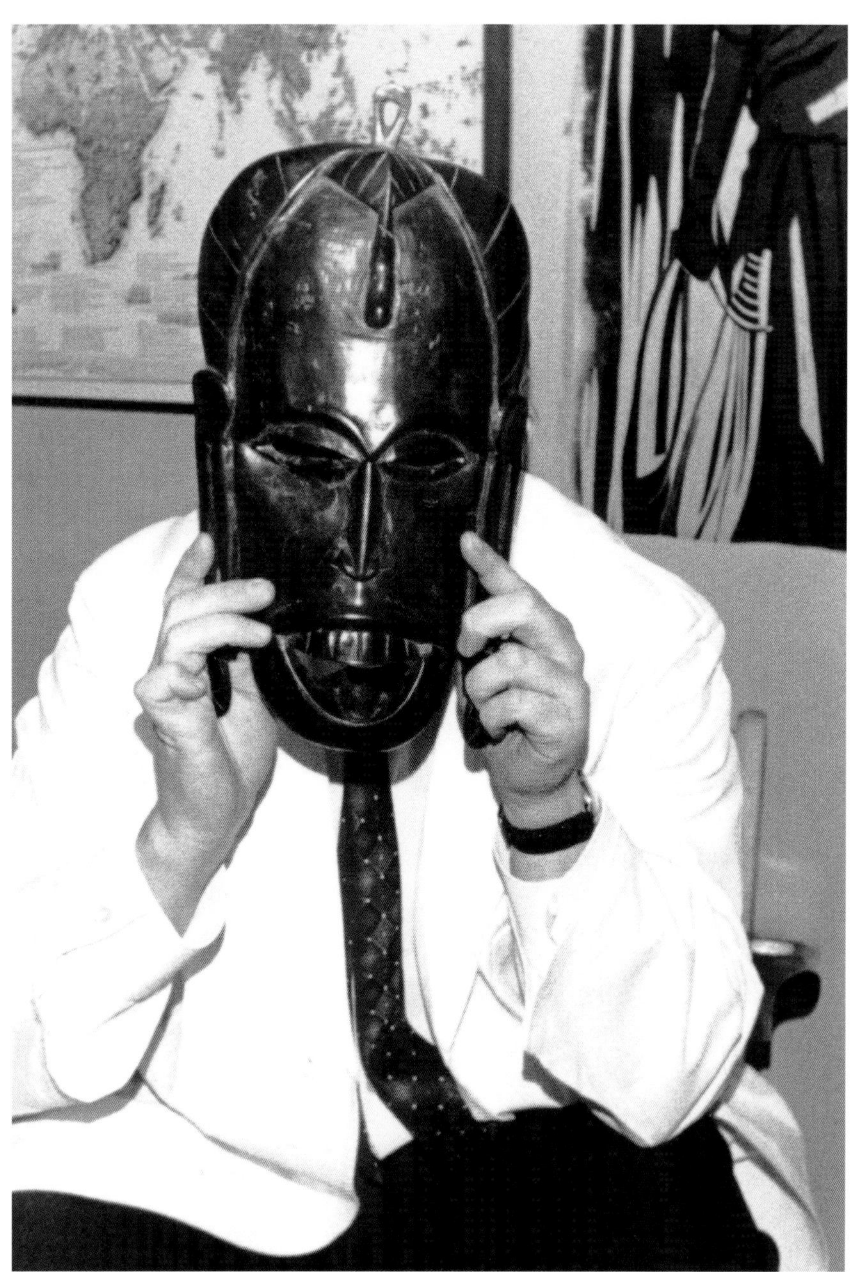

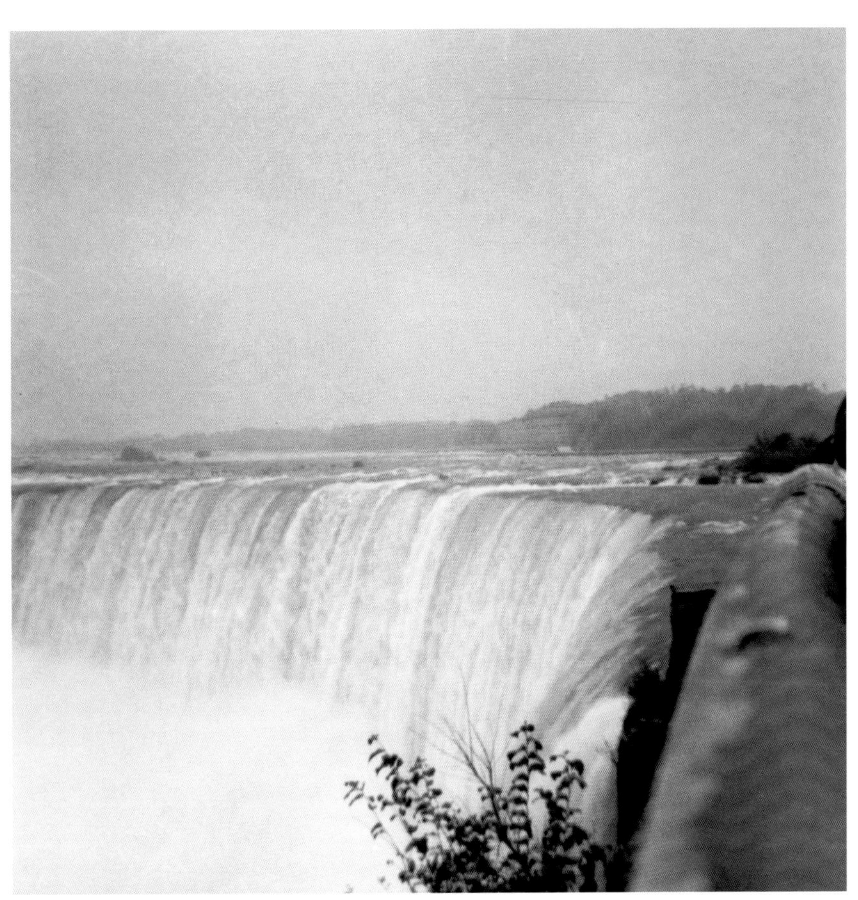

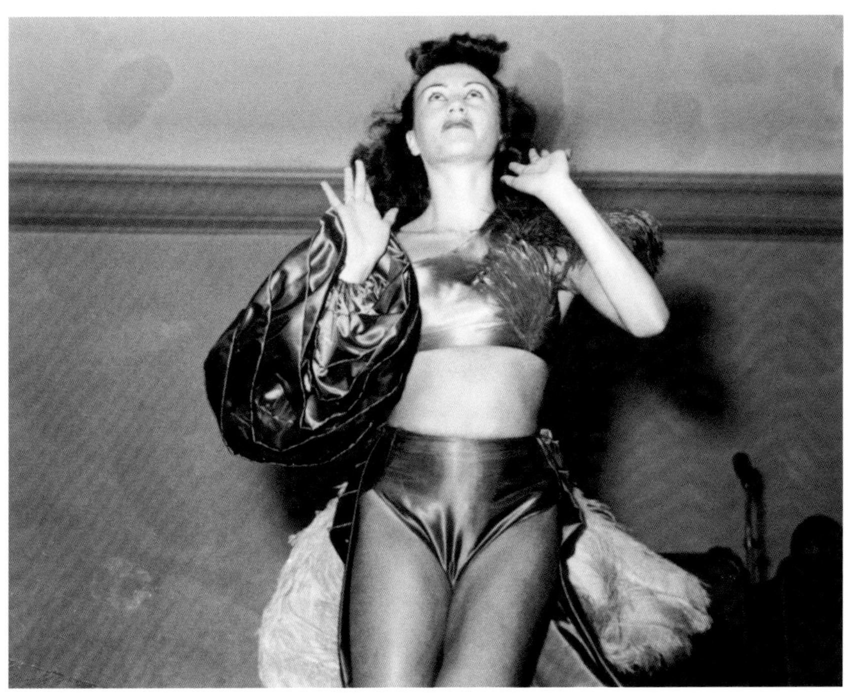

...she was breathing deeply, she forgot the cold, the weight of beings, the insane or static life, the long anguish of living or dying. After so many years running from fear, fleeing crazily, uselessly, she was finally coming to a halt. At the same time she seemed to be recovering her roots, and the sap rose anew in her body, which was no longer trembling. Pressing her whole belly against the parapet, leaning toward the wheeling sky, she was only waiting for her pounding heart to settle down, and for the silence to form in her. The last constellations of stars fell in bunches a little lower on the horizon of the desert, and stood motionless. Then, with an unbearable sweetness, the waters of the night began to fill her, submerging the cold, rising gradually to the center of her being, and overflowing wave upon wave to her moaning mouth. A moment later, the whole sky stretched out above her as she lay with her back against the cold earth...

—Albert Camus

DIVE DARK DREAM SLOW

All pictures from the collection of Peter J. Cohen
Edited by Melissa Catanese

Second printing March 2013

Coordination: Jacques Marlow
Distribution: D.A.P. // www.artbook.com
ISBN 978-0-9823653-7-3
Printed in China

THE ICE PLANT
PO Box 29247 Los Angeles CA 90029
www.theiceplant.cc